"If only this wonderful book were available when I was teaching directing. Great for the beginner, and a perfect refresher course in all the fundamentals for the experienced director. An invaluable guide for the journey from 'play to stage.'"

Gregory Lehane, *Professor Emeritus, and former Head of Directing at the Carnegie Mellon School of Drama*

"This indispensable guide to building an effective stage director's prompt book enables a director to approach production with a thorough understanding of the structure and detail of the play. It is a powerful template for creativity and collaboration."

Marc Masterson, *Former Artistic Director of Actors Theatre of Louisville and South Coast Repertory*

"Leslie Ferreira opens up the treasure chest of his knowledge, skill and experience as a stage director by sharing the playbook of his extraordinary craft. *The Stage Director's Prompt Book* is a *pièce de résistance* that brings everything together and takes your directing craft to the next level. Any director who seeks to up-their-game will immediately benefit from Leslie Ferreira's meticulous and creative approach to directing. This rare insight into directing is a gift of a lifetime that will keep on giving."

Eric Bishop, *Chair, Kennedy Center American College Theatre Festival, Region 8*

"Leslie Ferreira's *The Stage Director's Prompt Book* is the perfect companion for any director's journey. It offers encouragement, inspiration, and concrete advice—challenging us along the way to 'direct better.'"

Tina Kronis, *Artistic Director, Theatre Movement Bazaar*

"Why hasn't the *The Stage Director's Prompt Book* been written years ago? It clearly establishes the Who, What, Where, When, Why and How to effectively direct a play using the road map of a prompt book. Leslie Ferreira demystifies how to approach directing—all through the importance of the Three-Column Left-Hand Page. An excellent guide for anyone brave enough to call themselves, director."

Daniel T. Green, Ph.D., *Director: Entertainment Industry Management, Carnegie Mellon University*

"A great guide for assembling and organizing all the essential elements for a production, *The Stage Director's Prompt Book* is an excellent step-by-step method for investigating a play and developing a sound directorial approach to it."

Tom Bryant, *Dramaturg, Professor Emeritus, Crafton Hills College*

"A thoroughly entertaining, insightful and straightforward account of the steps needed to bring a play to life on stage. Not only directors but everyone else involved in the creation of theatre will benefit immeasurably from reading this book."

Anthony Maggio, *Chair, Theatre Academy, Los Angeles City College*

The Stage Director's Prompt Book

The Stage Director's Prompt Book is a step-by-step detailed guide on how to create a practical and powerful rehearsal and performance tool—the director's prompt book.

A prompt book is a coordinating and organizational tool for the stage director. This book systematizes the creative process the director uses to analyze and interpret a play and coordinates all director-related rehearsal and production activities into a single, self-contained interpretive and organizational system. This book guides the director through the necessary steps and stages of creating and using a prompt book—from play analysis and interpretation, through the formation of a dynamic and theatrical director's vision, to a unique method of physicalizing a play in production. A prompt book of a one-act play is included in the book as a complete example of the system. Such techniques as redlining, color coding and creating a three-column left-hand page are vividly illustrated for readers, allowing them to assemble their own prompt books. In a clear and example-driven format, *The Stage Director's Prompt Book* offers a system of directorial interpretation that takes the director through a series of point-by-point instructions to construct a strong, effective and creative instrument for success.

For the undergraduate and graduate students of theatre directing, stage management and producing courses, along with aspiring professional directors, this book provides an interactive and intuitive approach to personalize the stage directing experience and assemble a graphically dynamic and creative director's prompt book.

Leslie Ferreira is Professor Emeritus and former Chair of the Theater Arts Department and Producing Director of the Theatre Academy at Los Angeles City College. He is one of the most awarded directors in the history of the Kennedy Center American College Theatre Festival with over 20 national production awards, as well as the *Faculty Fellowship in Directing* for Outstanding Achievement as a Teaching Artist, the *Excellence in Theatre Education Award* and the prestigious *Gold Medallion* for his contributions to the teaching and producing of theatre. As a member of the Stage Directors and Choreographers, he has worked professionally as a stage director for over 40 years.

The Stage Director's Prompt Book

A Guide to Creating and Using the Stage Director's Most Powerful Rehearsal and Production Tool

Leslie Ferreira

NEW YORK AND LONDON

Designed cover image: © Shutterstock

First published 2023
by Routledge
605 Third Avenue, New York, NY 10158

and by Routledge
4 Park Square, Milton Park, Abingdon, Oxon, OX14 4RN

Routledge is an imprint of the Taylor & Francis Group, an informa business

© 2023 Taylor & Francis

The right of Leslie Ferreira to be identified as author of this work has been asserted in accordance with sections 77 and 78 of the Copyright, Designs and Patents Act 1988.

All rights reserved. No part of this book may be reprinted or reproduced or utilised in any form or by any electronic, mechanical, or other means, now known or hereafter invented, including photocopying and recording, or in any information storage or retrieval system, without permission in writing from the publishers.

Trademark notice: Product or corporate names may be trademarks or registered trademarks, and are used only for identification and explanation without intent to infringe.

Library of Congress Cataloging-in-Publication Data
Names: Ferreira, Leslie, author.
Title: The stage director's prompt book : a guide to creating and using the stage director's most powerful rehearsal and production tool / Leslie Ferreira.
Description: New York, NY : Routledge, 2023. | Includes index.
Identifiers: LCCN 2022031669 (print) | LCCN 2022031670 (ebook) | ISBN 9780367861070 (hardback) | ISBN 9780367861087 (paperback) | ISBN 9781003016946 (ebook)
Subjects: LCSH: Promptbooks | Theater--Production and direction--Handbooks, manuals, etc.
Classification: LCC PN2053 .F433 2023 (print) | LCC PN2053 (ebook) | DDC 792.02/33--dc23/eng/20221103
LC record available at https://lccn.loc.gov/2022031669
LC ebook record available at https://lccn.loc.gov/2022031670

ISBN: 978-0-367-86107-0 (hbk)
ISBN: 978-0-367-86108-7 (pbk)
ISBN: 978-1-003-01694-6 (ebk)

DOI: 10.4324/9781003016946

Typeset in Minion Pro and Avenir
by KnowledgeWorks Global Ltd.

To
My Teachers: Malcolm Bridges, Douglas Johnson, Lawrence Carra, Radu Penciulescu, Leon Katz and Milton Katselas

My Students

and
Barbara Foley Ferreira, Mara and Anthony

Contents

	About the Author	x
	Acknowledgments	xii
1	Introduction	1
2	A Director's Glossary: In Order of Appearance	6
3	The Mechanics of it All: Constructing the Prompt Book	16
4	Redlining the Script: Finding the Important, Distilling the Essence	22
5	Director's Units	25
6	Color Coding	28
7	The Three Column Left-Hand Page	31
8	The Right-Hand Page	35
9	Using the Prompt Book to Schedule and Organize for Artistic Success	37
10	The Director and the Stage Manager	66
11	Four One-Hundredths: A Model One Act	85
		126
		128

He directed the stage version of the Disney/Walden film *Holes* for Walden Entertainment in Denver, Colorado. In 2010, he participated in a grant from the National Endowment for the Arts directing *Bloody Red Heart* at the Odyssey Theatre Ensemble.

He was the Managing Director of the two-stage Equity theatre, Carnegie Mellon Theatre Company, and the Artistic and Producing Director for the Pittsburgh Park Players as well as a consultant to the Pennsylvania Council on the Arts. He has directed at such theatres as the Pittsburgh Public, Theatre Express, City Theatre Company, Actor's Alley, the Skylight, the Court and The Evidence Room.

He served for many years as an Ovation Voter for the Los Angeles Stage Alliance and has sat on the City of Los Angeles Cultural Affairs Department Grant Panel for Dance.

In 2009 the Kennedy Center/American College Theater Festival honored him with the *Faculty Fellowship in Directing* for Outstanding Achievement as a Teaching Artist and in 2014 he received the Kennedy Center American College Theater Festival *Excellence in Theatre Education Award*.

In 2022 Mr. Ferreira was honored by KCACTF with the Gold Medallion for his contributions to the teaching and producing of theatre. It is the most prestigious regional award given by KCACTF and is considered one of the great honors in theatre education.

Acknowledgments

Connor Clark Pasquale
Daniel Green
Richard Hellesen

For performance rights to *Four One-Hundredths,* contact the playwright at rshellesen@yahoo.com

CHAPTER 1

Introduction

The Stage Director's Prompt Book
is
An Organizational and Interpretative Creative System
A Coordinating and Organizing Tool
A Blueprint
A Road Map
A Guide
A Plan
A Compass
An Insurance Policy
A Cheat Sheet
A North Star
A Guiding Light
A Repository
A Storehouse
A Structural Method
A Research File
An Organizer
A Categorizer
A Database
A Monitor (of Intent, of Purpose, of Direction)
A Collaborative Instrument

The playwright creates the play. The director—in collaboration with many other artists—creates the production. The playwright writes the play. The director *constructs* the prompt book.

The prompt book contains the play but is not the play. Although it includes the playwright's words, the prompt book is actually much more than the play itself. It is the repository of all of the director's research, artistic ideas, musings, imaginings and plans for the play. It is, in short, the single most important tool that a director brings into the rehearsal room.

The director's prompt book is the place to investigate the text, and it is the place to organize one's analysis and interpretation. In essence, it is where a director truly discovers and finds the play. It is not just a three-ring binder with a copy of the play, the rehearsal schedule and some random notes.

A well-conceived and well-constructed prompt book is the best guarantee of a successful production. It is the guiding force that unites the director and the play, the director and the playwright, the director and the actors, the director and the designers—and, ultimately, the director and the audience.

This book is designed primarily for the beginning director, especially the undergraduate and graduate student of directing, but I hope that even the experienced director may find this book helpful. For the early student of directing, it provides a proven system and roadmap to get your creative ideas organized and implemented. For the more experienced director, it is a book that may provide an alternative path, another way of approaching the job. Its goal is to offer an approach for any director to better understand and interpret the play being directed, to clarify the director's artistic intent and to help the director communicate the deepest values of the play to an audience.

This is a practical, how to book—a book to *use* more than a book to merely read. Not unlike a cookbook, it offers a recipe to create a powerful, creative resource that will guide a director page-by-page, scene-by-scene and act-by-act through the rehearsal and production process.

The prompt book system presented here is a template that a director can use to physicalize a play onstage. A strong prompt book allows the director to organize the play for rehearsal, to make workable and theatrical sense of the playwright's words, and to arrange and structure the rehearsal process in an effective and meaningful way.

I created my first prompt book when I was 16 years old. I really had no idea what I was doing and had no real example. I was a junior in high school, a young actor with ambitions to direct. My high school drama teacher, Malcolm Bridges, had recently been rebuked by our school's principal for producing—in the eyes of the school's administration—some controversial and inappropriate one-act plays, and my mentor and drama teacher resigned in protest rather than be censored. What can I say? It was the late 1960s!

A ruling came down. There were to be no plays produced the following semester. So, I decided to make a proposal to the school. I would direct! And to prepare I picked a play, Tennessee Williams's *The Glass Menagerie*. Yes, I would direct, and I would cast four of my friends to play the parts. I wasn't asking for any money for production; I just wanted a space to rehearse and a commitment of a date to perform. In order to have the best chances of gaining the approval of the administration, I decided to present them with a prompt book that would prove my seriousness of purpose and demonstrate the promise of my success.

I had a copy of the play. The cover was a simple and subtle line drawing of intertwined animals—a menagerie. I tore the book's pages from their binding, got a ream of paper, cut a window in the middle of the paper, pasted rubber cement on the pages and mounted them onto the paper. This was before Xerox machines. I three-hole punched the paper and put it in a three-ring binder. I felt satisfied and almost like a real director. The prompt book was giving me confidence. I mean, if I can do this, I can direct. I made a few random notes here and there in the margins of the script, created some squiggly diagrams of possible set configurations, made some Xs to notate blocking moves, and was generally quite satisfied with myself and my efforts. My book was done.

Then I presented it to the school's administration, and it and I were unceremoniously and decidedly rejected. Ruling number two: No student was going to direct a play at Delta High School. That was my first experience with creating a prompt book—utter rejection. I don't think if Elia Kazan or Mike Nichols would have presented a prompt book the result would have been any different. I'm not sure my prompt book was even opened, much less read. Although I now know that my first prompt book was woefully inadequate, I did eventually find my way to create a more effective book.

Fast forward about ten years, I have graduated from undergraduate school at Berkeley and am sitting in my first MFA directing class at Carnegie Mellon University. First day of graduate school and I am assigned to direct a one-act play. It will go up in two weeks. I have 12 two-hour rehearsals to get the job done. In total, I have 24 hours of rehearsal time. I choose Luigi Pirandello's *The Man with the Flower in His Mouth*. It is cast for me; I have no say. I get busy on my prompt book. I vaguely remember being given a couple of mimeographed sheets with some vague outline of what I needed to present in terms of a prompt book. Minimal guidance.

The truth is I am deeply indebted and owe a great deal of gratitude to my teacher, Lawrence Carra. I was in awe of him before I met him. His seminal book, *Fundamentals of Play Direction*, was my undergraduate bible. My dream was to study and learn from him. Over his long career, thousands of actors heard him tell them to "sparkle" in his trademark Italian/Boston accent, and, indeed, he himself had a sparkling career. Born in Italy in 1909, Carra came to America with his family at the age of three. Without his knowledge, one of his high school teachers arranged for him to receive a full academic scholarship to Harvard, and he began to prepare to study medicine. His true passion, however, was the theatre. He directed plays for the

Harvard Drama Club, graduated in 1931 and, after a miserable year of medical school in Rome, returned to America and enrolled in the Yale School of Drama. At Yale, Carra did research for a young professor, Alexander Dean, who was working on a directing book. The first edition of *Fundamentals of Play Directing*, first published in 1941, became the leading college text used to train stage directors, but Alexander Dean died two years earlier, at the age of 46, before the book was published. Larry finished the book and became the co-author for all succeeding editions.

When I applied to graduate school, I had to send a photo of myself in with my application. A friend of mine's father worked for Polaroid, and his father would send him prototype cameras and cartons of Instamatic film. In his apartment he positioned me in front of a bookcase crammed full of books, and I artfully placed *Fundamentals of Play Directing* on a shelf so that it appeared as though the book was actually leaping out of my head. (I was going for the subtle subliminal directorial effect.) When I had my interview with Larry at the American Conservatory Theatre in San Francisco, and he asked me why I wanted to be a director I said, not too artfully, that I wanted to "control" what was on stage. I didn't know it at the time, but Larry was working on a second book, *Controls in Play Directing*, and his major theme of that book was to apply the previous book's fundamentals in specific ways to "control" for genre and individual effect. I don't know if it was the subliminal use of the Polaroid Instamatic shot of me grinning with his book in the background, or my lucky word choice in the interview, but I was accepted.

At Carnegie, Larry was Lorenzo the Great to the grad directors. He carried a handful of yellowed, handwritten lecture notes that served as a reminder that he had been teaching for over 30 years, and that what he had to say was important enough to be written down so he wouldn't forget to say it. I was in his last class of directors, one of three of his final students. We learned the "Fundies."

He taught me to sit in the back row—to better see the stage as a director—and as an audience member might—in the worst seats in the house. If it can play to the last row—and to the sides of the house—it can play. He talked about the "little, old, deaf lady" in the back row and would ask if she could hear the dialogue. One of his fabled notes to actors was, "Act Better." On first exposure to that note, one might think of it as crude or condescending or even cruel. But Larry was none of those things. He was elegant and humble and ever kind. The note, "Act Better," delivered with an omnipresent smile on his face, is brilliant in its way; it allows the actor to ponder and to discover how to be better. "How can I be better?" is a great question for an actor, any artist, to ask. It gives the actor the actual freedom to improve in his or her own way. Much better than "faster," "louder." And it's not a bad question for directors either. I tell my directing students a variation of Larry's line: "Direct Better."

And that starts with the quality of a director's prompt book.

Larry taught me how to create a better prompt book, certainly a better version than my early effort with *The Glass Menagerie*. The system I present in this book is a variation of a similar system I learned from Larry Carra. From him I inherited the left- and right-hand page structure and the three-column divisions. What I have attempted to do is to codify and clarify, to expand and enhance, what he first presented to me as a way to organize a director's prompt book. Larry died, at the age of 97, in 2006. It was an honor to have been his student, and I am ever grateful for the many lessons he taught me.

I hope this book and the system I present will allow directors to structure their work in both effective and creative ways. I should also mention that the prompt book you create will not necessarily be exactly the same as the one I present in this book. All prompt books bear the personal stamp of their directors. No two are the same. Each book is unique and an intimate expression of the individual director's creativity. Remember that prompt books are handmade so they carry all of the blemishes and imperfections of something hand-crafted. Don't worry if your book is a little messy or cluttered with a crazy scrawl only you can interpret. The system I present is a way to order and organize, yes, but not to confine and overly define your directorial expression. The important thing is to make your prompt book your own—your own effective tool for successfully directing the play.

CHAPTER 2

A Director's Glossary: In Order of Appearance

In Arthur Miller's landmark American classic, *Death of a Salesman*, Willy Loman's widow, Linda, speaks the line, "Attention must be paid." It is her mourning command as to what is owed her dead husband.

The Zen master Ikkyu was once asked to write a distillation of the highest wisdom. He wrote only one word: Attention. His visitor was displeased. "Is that all?" So Ikkyu obliged him. Two words now. *Attention. Attention.*

The key to directing is paying attention.

Directing is a form of meditation. Meditation takes many forms, and one of them is the placing of attention on an object. Like a mantra, a candle, an icon or the breath, the play on the page and the play in rehearsal and performance are the meditative objects on which directors must focus their attention. As you read the play, as you watch and listen in rehearsal, you must attend to what is before you.

First step, pick up the play and go through it, page by page. Read it. We're trying to identify its component parts and to see how they all fit together and what they all mean. Some of these elements will be obvious, others will be hidden. Some will be easy to find and track, others will take some searching. But these are the ingredients that need to be isolated, considered and attended to inside the prompt book. These are the dramaturgical, meditative objects to which you must bring your directorial attention. One read won't do it. It will take several passes for the play to make itself known. You want more than a first date; you want a relationship.

One of the strongest pieces of advice I give directors is to read the play. *Read the Play. Read the Play. Read the Play.* Most questions are answered by reading the play. A director needs to read the play with attentive intelligence. A play, especially a complex one, rarely reveals itself all at once, but more commonly, slowly and gradually. It's like a long-cooked dish, we have to read the play, let it marinate, simmer in our brains, stew a bit, before we can fully appreciate its richness, its full meaning and its multiple secrets. Yes, attention must be paid.

Let's take a look at some of the fundamental elements of every play. We need to be on the lookout for these elements and their deeper meanings.

I've organized this director's glossary, not in alphabetical order, but rather in the rough "order of appearance" as you will find them when you start to read the script.

Title: The playwright titled the play. What does the title of the play signify? Why this title? What insight can be gleamed from an investigation of the play's title? Do this: Look up every word of the title in a good dictionary and see what comes up. Spend some time contemplating the title.

Playwright: Read the playwright's other plays. You'd be surprised at what you will discover. Many playwrights often have subjects, themes, types of characters and concerns that show up in more than one of their works. By reading deeply from the other plays they have written, you have a leg up on understanding the play you are directing. The playwright Stephen Adly Guirgis, for example, has written many plays with characters who are Catholic, are alcoholics, are New Yorkers. His common themes are forgiveness and redemption. If you are directing his *Our Lady of 121st Street*, reading any of his other plays will help you increase your understanding of the one you are directing.

Production History: Look in the front of the play for the original cast list and production credits. This will tell you not only when the play was first performed, but who played each part, who directed it and where it was produced. Armed with this you can start to understand the production's history and gain insight into casting, design and interpretation. A director should not live in ignorance of a production's history or how other directors have approached the play. You may be challenged to reevaluate your own precious ideas. You may be confirmed in your judgment. But it can be a foolish and arrogant mistake not to know how other directors have approached the play or what other smart minds have had to say about it. To avoid knowing about the work of previous directors is to live in ignorance. Don't be afraid; this knowledge won't pollute your own vision.

Cast of Characters: What is the playwright telling you about the play right up front by using these characters to tell the story? What about the actual names of the characters the playwright has chosen? Do the names indicate anything special? Are ages indicated or are there other salient characteristics mentioned?

The Setting: Is there information about the setting provided that needs extra attention? The setting will affect the design, the budget, the lighting and costumes. And it will affect your blocking and staging decisions.

Inciting Incident(s): Sometimes also referred to as the Precipitating Event or the Fuse Event or the Ignition Event. This is a pre-curtain event that starts the dramatic action. It isn't inside the play proper but precedes the play. In *Hamlet* it would be the murder of Hamlet's father, the marriage of his mother to his uncle and the appearance of the ghost. All of these events occurred before the first line of dialogue. These are very important events to identify and get right because they will unlock many other elements of the play.

Plot: Aristotle put plot at the top of his hit parade of a play's key elements. We are talking about the story, the narrative. As a director you have to know the story. You can't tell a story you don't know. What happens? What happens next? Look for the cause-and-effect relationship between events. You'll have to write it out. Unit by unit, event by event. And only focus on the on-stage action, what the audience will actually experience. We'll call this your Plot Outline. More on this later.

The Character Five: Write out five key words for each character. Focus on the fundamental words that define the essential nature of the character. These words could be nouns or adjectives or, to fudge, even short phrases. The important thing is to distill the character into their basic and indispensable qualities—especially as how they function in terms of story and emotion.

Here's an example:

Hamlet: Son. Avenger. Indecisive. Melancholic. Prince.

Each director will have their own list. The actor will have their own list. But it's important for the director to start the process by identifying those aspects of character that are essential to communicate in order to fully express the character and the play. And this has to be done before casting. It is essential to go into the casting process having an understanding of the play's characters. How else could you accurately and appropriately cast the play?

Given Circumstances: One of the best short-hand tools for a director to keep the production honest. These are sometimes referred to as the five Ws and the H. Where, When, What, Who, Why and How. You have to define these or you risk violating the basic reality of the play's world. Be as specific as you can be. Write them down. These Givens may change from scene to scene or act to act. Sometimes they can even change within a scene. They affect everything.

Where: This Given Circumstance is akin to a dramaturgical GPS. It zeros in on place—where, in space, a play occurs.
PLANET EARTH>UNITED STATES>LOS ANGELES>HOLLYWOOD>SUNSET BOULEVARD>APARTMENT BUILDING>THIRD FLOOR, REAR>LIVING ROOM.

A play may have many Wheres; each scene may be different or there may even be split locations within the same scene. You need to account for them all.

When: If, in the play's time/space continuum the Where is the space, the When is the time. When does the play take place?
1952 > LATE NOVEMBER, A FRIDAY NIGHT, 3:23 AM.

Again, a play can have many Whens, a range of times that may shift and change for every scene, or even within a scene. The combination of the Whens and the Wheres will affect all design decisions, especially the costume and lighting designs. December in Los Angeles is different from December in London. 1:00 AM on a Saturday night is different from 1:00 PM on a Tuesday afternoon.

What is about event. It can shift from scene to scene and even within scenes. There can also be an overriding expression of the What for the entire play; *Hamlet* could be distilled down to A Revenge. In essence, we are asking the question, "What's happening?" What's the onstage action? Really? Try to describe it as a noun not a verb. A Confession. A Business Proposal. A Theft. An Attack. How can you uncover the most dramatic possible sense of the event in the fewest possible words? Distill it down to its essential dramatic nature. Each director unit's event has a What that should be defined.

Who is all about Character, the people of the play. Define the characters by starting with a CHARACTER FIVE list for each character in the play. Go further and write a biography for each major character. The director will collaborate with the actor on the development of character, but it is important for the director to have a deep understanding of the play's characters and at the same time recognize that it will be the actors who will ultimately communicate the characters to the audience.

Why is about the reasons the characters do what they do. Just simply ask yourself why are the characters acting and behaving the way they are. What do they want? The Why unlocks their objectives, their motivations, and their intentions in the purest possible way.

How reveals the way and manner in which characters achieve their objectives. The How modifies the Why. It's what they *do* to get what they *want*. One may pout or one may scream to get the same thing. This may be specified in the action of the play by the playwright or invented by the director or the actor or even inspired by another member of the creative team. It's what the audience hears and sees the characters do to achieve their goals. It defines both the characters and the action of the play.

Subject/Theme/Thought: This is the intellectual underpinnings of the play. Basically, what's the play about? Here we're focused more on idea than on action. Start with an abstract sense of the subject. Make a long list, then zero in on one or two main, key subjects. It could be Justice, Revenge, Loyalty. Then try to understand what the playwright is saying, specifically *through the play's action*, about the subject matter. That's the theme. The subject of a play can be a single word, but not the theme. Theme is not a single word; one word is not a theme. Justice is a subject; "No Justice, No Peace" is a theme. Revenge is a subject; "Revenge is Sweet" is a theme. Loyalty is a subject; "There is no loyalty among thieves" is a theme. Most importantly, the onstage action *must* support and bear out both the subject and the theme.

Exposition: Information the audience needs to know about past events that affect the life of the play. Exposition often exists at the beginning of a play or the beginning of an act. It fills in the blanks for the audience and provides them with the information and context to follow and track the theatrical journey—describing past events that occurred before the play began and outside of the onstage action of the play, and, sometimes, between events inside the play itself. Exposition points backward in time.

Foreshadowing: Any indication of a future event, foreshadowing points forward in time. Chekhov's famous gun in act one that must go off in act three is a prime example. It is an inherently dramatic literary device that builds conscious and, often, unconscious tension and suspense. It begs the question, "What if…?" It hints at future action and thus creates a sense of expectation on the part of the audience. It puts questions in audience's minds. "Will the bomb explode?" "Will they find the pot of gold?" "Will they kiss?" And when foreshadowed events finally occur it creates a sense of satisfaction for the playgoer. I knew it! I told you so!

Dialogue/Language/Diction: Two of the principal ways a play communicates is through physical action and verbal action. Dialogue is the verbal action. Investigate the language. Is it prose or verse? Is it formal or colloquial? Is it poetic or mundane? Is it spoken with a dialect? How does it contribute to the style of the play? What does it say about the characters, their class, their education, their status? How does it affect the rhythm of the play?

Look up any word you don't know the definition of and make sure you know the proper pronunciation of all of the words in the play.

Music/Sounds of the Play: Anything and everything you hear in the course of the playgoing experience. Anything and everything. Dialogue, the sound of the actors' voices and the very words themselves, are all part of the music. So are the phone ring, car horn and fiddle in the wings. So is the preshow music. As a director you need to be sensitive to what the audience hears. You need to know when this music, these sounds, enter and exit the play and how they contribute to the overall communication of the play. A close reading of script, your analysis and interpretation, will lead you to better collaborations with your designers as you work together to find the truths embedded in the script and to realize these elements of the play.

Spectacle/Sights of the Play: Anything and everything you see in the course of the playgoing experience. Anything and everything. The actors' bodies standing on the stage, the actors' bodies moving across the stage. The costumes, the scenery, the props, the lighting. The hair and makeup. The architecture of the theater itself. Confucius said "a picture is worth a thousand words" and in the theatre, being a most visual artform, so much is experienced through the eyes of the spectator. How can what an audience sees influence their interpretation of the play? How can what an audience senses through their eyes tell the story, shape their understanding of the characters and affect their emotional response to the play? Rock legend Rod Stewart has a song, *Every Picture Tells a Story.* That's great advice for a director.

Cues: Lights, Sounds, Projections, Moving Scenery, Special Effects. They all need to be accounted for in the Prompt Book. They are communications too! They can create tone and mood; they can support subject and theme; they can affect audience response. Cues have entrances and exits just as characters do, and thus a director needs to pay special attention to when cues begin and when cues end. Many will be immediately known and found through reading the script. Others will be developed in rehearsal and found through collaboration with the actors and designers.

Protagonist: Who's the main character? Who is affected the most by the play's action? Who are we tracking, following most closely? Who do we care about and empathize with the most? Who is present at almost all of the major happenings of the play? In most plays it is a single character, but not all. We have *Romeo and Juliet*—an example of dual protagonists. Sometimes it's a group of people—as in *Waiting for Lefty*. But usually, it's one character. Sometimes you can tell by the title of the play—*Hamlet, King Lear, Othello*. But even then, there is debate. There are plenty of people who will interpret Othello as a play with Iago as the protagonist. What's important is that you decide. And direct the play accordingly. Make sure the audience follows and tracks your protagonist's journey from inciting incident to point of attack to climax to resolution.

Protagonist's Goal: What does this character want? What is his or her overriding objective that arcs over the entire play. In *Hamlet* it could be stated as "to avenge his father's death." In *Streetcar Named Desire*, it is Blanche's objective to "find safety and security with her sister."

Antagonist: Who opposes the protagonist? Who blocks the protagonist from achieving their goal? If Stella is the protagonist of *A Streetcar Named Desire*, then Stanley is her antagonist. Hamlet, Claudius. Batman, Joker. Sometimes there can be more than one antagonist. Sometimes the antagonist can even be an abstract concept or institution—like injustice, poverty, the system or the government. It can even be a force of nature, as in *Riders to the Sea*, a play about a mother who loses her fisherman sons, and the play's title reveals the answer; she loses her sons to the sea, the play's ancient antagonist.

Point of Attack: This is the first scene in the play that starts the true action of the play. It's usually an early scene. The protagonist is usually present. It's the first time we, as the audience, have the beginning understanding of what we are watching. It sets the play's true action in motion. It allows the audience to track the story. In this scene the direction of the plot begins to form, and we understand what we are waiting to find out. The protagonist takes his or her first step toward their ultimate goal. For example, in *Hamlet*, we have a clear point of attack scene, when the young *Hamlet* encounters the ghost of his father for the first time, learns of his foul murder—and vows to avenge his father's death. Or when Blanche Dubois arrives on her sister's doorstep in *A Streetcar Named Desire* and asks to be taken in, protected and given a home. In both these examples we have a clear sense of direction for the characters; they have both effectively set their courses of action that will lead to all of plays' complications, and ultimately, to each of the plays' climaxes.

Complications: A complication is anything that impedes the protagonist from achieving their goal. OBSTACLES and REVERSALS are subcategories of complications. This is where the true drama exists because complications inherently provide conflict, and conflict is the lifeblood of the drama.

> *Obstacle*: A major block to the achievement of an objective, something that must be overcome. Like an obstacle in the middle of the road, you must go over it, under it or around it. The character must do the same thing with the obstacles they face; they must shift and try a new tactic to get their objective.

> *Reversal*: A sharp setback that spins the character backward. A 180-degree turn in pursuit of the objective.

Crisis: The biggest complication prior to—and the one that propels us toward—the climax. It is the point of no return that leads us straight to the climactic scene. The rape scene in *A Streetcar Named Desire* inexorably leads us to the scene when the doctor arrives to take Blanche away. The dumbshow in *Hamlet* that proves Claudius's guilt leads us directly to *Hamlet* taking action, stabbing Claudius—and avenging his father's death.

Climax: The high point of the drama. Where all of the dramatic energy is finally expended and the play's argument is complete, its questions answered, and the protagonist's goals are achieved or denied and we are about to have the house lights come up.

Resolution: The tying up of all the loose ends. The resolving of the plot points. Usually, it's the scene after the climax.

The Play's Main Dramatic Question: Most plays center around some action that we await. Thus, a question arises in the minds of the audience. Will it happen or not? Will Romeo and Juliet's love survive? Will *Hamlet* avenge his father's death? Will Blanche find safe haven with her sister Stella? It's the concern, the main issue that keeps us in our seats, waiting to see if it will happen or not. Will Batman save Gotham from the Joker?

The Play's Main Statement: This is a shorthand distillation of the play's dramatic action. Sort of like a log line for a movie or television show, but even more precisely true to the onstage action. It can be created almost as a fill-in-the-blank statement.

This is a _____ about a _____ who _____ by _____.

Here is an example:

> This is a TRAGEDY about a young, indecisive, melancholic Danish PRINCE who AVENGES HIS FATHER'S DEATH by STAGING A DUMB SHOW that confirms the guilt of the murderer, and then KILLS HIS HOMICIDAL, STEP-FATHER UNCLE.

Mood: Mood is a feeling. It can also be a state of mind, an emotional state, or a defining spirit. In the theatre we can start by thinking of the two basic moods as being either comic or dramatic. We can also interpret moods in terms of lighter moods or heavier moods. Creating proper moods are important as they convey feelings to the audience in subtle yet powerful ways. The use of music can often help create moods or feelings very effectively and efficiently. Play dark and somber music and we create one mood; play bright and cheerful music and we create another.

Tone: The overall attitude toward or feelings about the subject matter. Mood shifts and changes from director's unit to director's unit, sometimes even within units. Mood is specific. Tone is general. Tone tends to permeate an entire work. We can start with the great dichotomy in drama, as represented in the masks of Melpomene and Thalia, the masks of tragedy and comedy. An easy first choice is to decide if the tone is comic or dramatic. Another way to look at it is thinking on a scale of value moving from light to heavy. It can be very helpful for a director to assess the tone of a play and to maintain the proper tone value of the play.

Style: Style is a way of doing something. Style can be a technique or a specific method of doing something. Style can reflect a genre as in musical styles—rap, reggae, country, pop, rock, etc. Primarily, it is the specific quality, method, form and approach artists take in communicating their work. A director needs to have a strong sense of the style of production and work to be consistent in its use and application. Some plays may be staged to limit or minimize a director's personal style; other plays may be staged to showcase and emphasize a directorial style. Directors such as Robert Wilson or Tadashi Suzuki both express themselves through highly individual and personal directorial styles.

Once we have identified the parts of the play and these salient elements, we are prepared to begin the assembly process of putting this knowledge to work in rehearsal—and in the prompt book. Your ideas may shift and change, be altered and adjusted by your interactions and collaborations with the creative team of actors and designers. There will be discoveries and revelations about that play that will only come through rehearsal and experimentation. It's a journey with a destination not completely known. There is rarely a "true north" when it comes to a play. There is rarely a direct route without certain detours. A well-designed prompt book, however, is the best insurance policy for a successful passage from first read of a script to opening night.

If you hold your focus, your attention, your meditative grip on the play—and develop the quality and strength of your prompt book—you will begin to see the play unfold, revealing its secrets, and, ultimately, finding its physical life on stage.

By beginning the process of analysis and interpretation and placing your hard-won insights about the play inside your prompt book, you gain increased authority over the production and a greater understanding of its mysteries and its potential to communicate itself to an audience.

CHAPTER 3

The Mechanics of It All: Constructing the Prompt Book

The great German-born, American architect and designer Mies Van der Rohe most famously said that "God is in the details," and for a stage director this is a reminder that every detail of a play's production becomes significant. The way the details get discovered—and then managed—is inside the Prompt Book.

The painter Vincent van Gogh, in a letter to his brother, Theo, said, "Great things are done by a series of small things brought together." Nothing can be truer for a stage director.

The first of the small things the director needs to do is to actually construct a physical prompt book. It is inside this prompt book where much of the work of the stage director will be done.

We're going to do this like a recipe.

Here are the ingredients you will need to bring together in order to create your book:

A Copy of the Play
A Three-ring Binder
A Set of Tabbed Dividers
A Three Hole Punch
A Box of Colored, *Erasable* Pencils
8.5 × 11-inch Paper
A Ruler

I like to have a physical, hard copy book rather than a digital prompt book because, although there are some advantages to electronic formats, there is something more visceral and flexible in a physical prompt book. If, however, you prefer to carry yours on your iPad or computer, feel free to adapt the content to the digital format.

1. If you have the publisher's permission, photocopy the script so that only one page of dialogue is centered and copied vertically on each sheet of paper. (You may consider increasing the size of the font when copying for easier reading.) Insert these pages into your three-ring binder; they now become your DIRECTOR'S RIGHT HAND PAGE.
(If you do not have the publisher's permission to photocopy you will need to buy two copies of the script, cut the pages out and mount each page individually on a separate piece of 8.5 × 11 paper using tape or paper mounting adhesive.)

    If you are working with an original script, you can proceed to copy the pages and insert them in your three-ring binder.
2. On each page opposite a dialogue page make three vertically running columns. Do *not* insert an extra page of paper between dialogue pages. You will be drawing your columns on the backside of the previous dialogue page. (Refer to the chapter on The Three Columns for a complete explanation of the DIRECTOR'S LEFT HAND PAGE.)
3. Behind the script place your dividers. Label one divider RESEARCH. In this section of the prompt book include all of the researched information you've discovered about the play. This could be critical articles, reviews, the bio of the playwright, images of locales pertinent to the play, etc. You may also receive valuable information from a dramaturg that would be placed behind this tab.
4. Label the next divider PLOT/STRUCTURE. In this section of the prompt book place your PLOT OUTLINE and other pertinent dramaturgical information. You will later transfer some of this significant information to the appropriate place in the script on the DIRECTOR'S LEFT HAND PAGE, primarily in COLUMN ONE.
5. Label one divider CHARACTER. In this section of the prompt book include information about the characters. This might include character biographies that you have written or images that you have collected that inspire you about the characters and that may be shared with the actors or designers. (Again, transfer the significant information discovered to the appropriate place in the script on the DIRECTOR'S LEFT HAND PAGE, primarily in COLUMN TWO.)
6. Label one divider MUSIC/SPECTACLE. In this section of the prompt book include information about what is seen and what is heard. This will

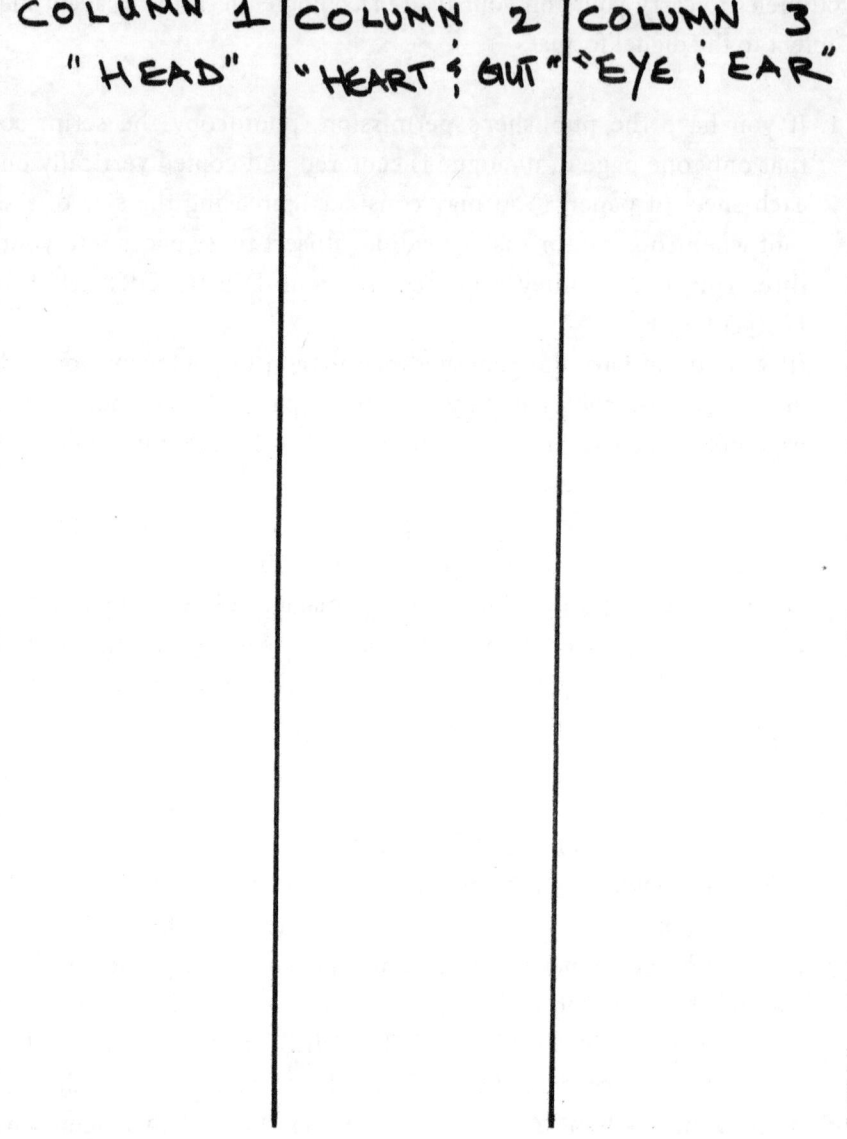

Figure 3.1 Blank three column left-hand page.

be visual images and sound/music references. (Transfer the significant information to the appropriate place in the script on the DIRECTOR'S LEFT HAND PAGE, primarily in COLUMN THREE.)

7. Label one tab GROUND PLAN. Place a copy of the ground plan(s) here.
8. Label one tab SCENERY. Place any notes on design that you wish to communicate to the scenic designer. Include any inspirational images, ideas about color, all scenic design plots and lists given to you by the designers, etc.
9. Label one tab COSTUMES. Place any images or notes on design that you wish to communicate to the costume designer. Include all costume plots,

including costume sketches in color, makeup suggestions, inspirational images, as provided by the costume designer.
10. Label one tab LIGHTING. Place any images or notes on design that you wish to communicate to the lighting designer. Include any comments on concept and mood as well as the light plot provided by the lighting designer.
11. Label one tab SOUND. Place any notes on design that you wish to communicate to the sound designer. Include all sound and music cues and the sound plot provided by the sound designer.
12. Label one tab PROPERTIES. Include the complete prop plot and any pertinent prop specific design images or notes.
13. Label one tab AUDITION MATERIALS. Include audition passages you will use, extra copies of the form or questionnaire you will ask performers to complete at auditions and copies of informational materials to be given to performers. Some of this may be provided by the theatre or casting director.
14. Label one tab REHEARSAL SCHEDULE. Include a detailed rehearsal.
15. Label one tab REHEARSAL REPORTS. File your daily reports here as provided by stage management.
16. Label one tab PRODUCTION MEETINGS. File your production meeting notes and reports here.
17. Label one tab BUSINESS. In this section place records of expenses and copies of correspondence regarding royalties and rights.
18. Label one tab GOALS. (Record goals for each rehearsal.)
19. Label one tab JOURNAL. This section will contain your personal record of each rehearsal.

In Chapter 4, Redlining the Script, you will learn the technique of scoring the important lines of dialogue or stage direction in red pencil.

Chapter 5 will introduce you to the technique of dividing the script into Director's Units, and in Chapter 6, Color Coding Your Script, you will learn how to go through your script with the colored pencils and color-mark your Prompt Book.

THREE COLUMN WORK

More detailed information on the three-column structure will be provided in subsequent chapters, but here is a quick overview:

1. On the left-hand pages, make sure each page is divided into three vertically running columns. Fill in the LEFT COLUMN with the pertinent

information: Your running critical commentary as described in Chapter 7.
2. Make sure you have divided the script into the appropriate **DIRECTOR'S UNITS** with a horizontal line drawn across both the left- and the right-hand pages. These units are key to unlocking the play's structure and form the basis for many directorial decisions. Base your divisions on shifts of *event* as they occur onstage as discussed in upcoming chapters.
3. In the CENTER COLUMN, number and give each Director's Unit a definitive **TITLE** that describes what happens in that unit. Think of the *noun* that defines the event. For example, A Confession, A Proposal, An Arrest, etc.
4. Under the title, write the **SCENE PURPOSE** of each Director's Unit.
5. Define the inherent **MOOD** in each unit.
6. In the CENTER COLUMN list each character in the action unit, their **CHARACTER OBJECTIVES** and character **ADJECTIVES/ ADVERBS**.
7. Fill in RIGHT COLUMN with the appropriate information regarding music and spectacle. Maintain the consistency of the color coding:

IMPORTANT LINES OF DIALOGUE OR STAGE DIRECTION in **RED** PENCIL
SOUND CUES in **ORANGE** PENCIL
LIGHT CUES in **DARK BLUE** PENCIL
SCENIC CUES in **GREEN** PENCIL
PROPERTIES in **VIOLET** PENCIL
COSTUMES in **YELLOW** PENCIL

8. Place your PRELIMINARY BLOCKING on the right-hand dialogue page directly connected to the dialogue line or line of stage directions on which the blocking takes place.
9. Place technical cues in the right-hand page's right margin.

See Chapter 8 for more details on creating your right-hand page.

THREE COLUMN LEFT-HAND PAGE FOR DIRECTORS		
RUNNING CRITICAL COMMENTARY	**DIRECTOR'S ACTION UNITS AND CHARACTER OBJECTIVES**	**SPECTACLE/ MUSIC**
HEAD/MIND	*HEART/GUT*	*EYE/EAR*
Quotes	DIRECTOR UNIT NUMBER	NOTES ON
Literary Criticism	TITLE/EVENT	• SCENERY
Pronunciations and Definitions	SCENE PURPOSE	• PROPERTIES
	INHERENT MOOD	• COSTUMES
Thought	CHARACTER OBJECTIVES	• LIGHTING
Interpretation	CHARACTER ADJECTIVES	• PROJECTIONS
Analysis	CHARACTER ADVERBS	• SOUND/MUSIC
Thematic Statements	....	(*NOT CUES*)
Comments on Period and Style	(Above Repeated for Every New Unit)	DIAGRAMS OF MOVEMENT
(Above Repeated for Every New Unit)	*Character Objectives May Shift and Adjust within Each Director Unit*	(*NOT BLOCKING NOTES*)
General Research		SKETCHES OF SET AND GROUNDPLANS

EACH UNIT SHOULD DIVIDE ACROSS BOTH LEFT AND RIGHT PAGES OF SCRIPT IN A SINGLE LINE.

DRAW A SOLID LINE FROM FAR LEFT ACROSS TO FAR RIGHT ON BOTH THE LEFT AND RIGHT PAGE OF THE SCRIPT. BLOCKING SHOULD BE PLACED ON THE RIGHT-HAND DIALOGUE PAGE DIRECTLY KEYED TO THE APPROPRIATE LINE OF DIALOGUE OR STAGE DIRECTION. TECHNICAL CUES ARE PLACED IN THE RIGHT-HAND PAGE'S RIGHT MARGIN.

CHAPTER 4

Redlining the Script: Finding the Important, Distilling the Essence

I'm going to start with two stories of distillation, one from the world of advertising, the other from the world of literary fiction.

When the German automaker BMW introduced its new BMW 1 Series car in the United States in 2004, they took out billboards that featured the, new-to-America, tiny car. The executives at the car company weren't sure how the American consumer would accept a super small subcompact BMW. The billboards were simple, just the image of the car and this single line of ad copy: *Distilled, Yet Never Reduced.*

Here's the other story. The American novelist Ernest Hemingway walked into El Floridita bar in Havana, Cuba and ordered a daiquiri. Or so the story goes. A man at the bar challenged the famous author to write a novel using only six words. Before the bartender could set down Hemingway's drink, or perhaps after he had consumed more than one, he came up with this: "For Sale: Baby Shoes, Never Worn."

That's distillation. Four words that sell a car. Six words that capture and tell a story. All art is, in essence, a distillation. The play's story may span decades, and yet the play is over in less than two hours. The art of the theatre is the art of compression. One of the director's first tasks is to understand the nature of compression and to understand *the essential*—that which is emphatic and requires highlighting and the attention of the audience.

That's where redlining comes in. Redlining is a technique. It allows the director to see more clearly the essential nature of the action of the play, to perceive the important and to distinguish the primary.

Here's how it's done. After you've already read the script two or three times, grab a red, erasable pencil. Start reading the play again. Slowly. Be open and sensitive to lines of dialogue and lines of stage direction that are, in essence, essential. These are the hot lines—our redlines. Lines that cannot be ignored, lines that cannot be omitted. Lines that burn a little brighter than others, ones that carry dramatic energy and theatrical heat.

These are lines of dialogue and/or lines of stage direction that, if they weren't in the script, the play would not be the play that it is. We can't cut them out. If we do, we lose the play.

Be on the lookout for lines that do primarily three things: Give us key information about the *plot*, provide insight into the truest nature of the *characters*, and shed light on the *emotional* life and mood of the play.

Once you find these lines, underline them in red. That's redlining.

But…don't go to Redline Heaven—where every other line is underlined. Redlining means nothing if everything is redlined. If everything is emphasized nothing is emphasized. Search out only the key lines of dialogue and the key lines of stage direction, the ones that truly define and propel the play.

It's not that all the lines that are not redlined are unimportant. It's not that they are unnecessary. But there can be nothing emphatic if everything is of the same value. It's like an actor yelling through the lines of a monologue. After a while it all sounds the same, sound and fury signifying nothing. When this happens, everything *is* the same and nothing stands out.

One of the first things a director has to do is find out what is most important and what, most importantly, is not. Redlining is the first step in that process.

We're trying to distill, not reduce, just like BMW when they introduced that 1 series into the American market. A tiny, little car was not part of its portfolio of automobiles nor a type of car associated with their brand in America. That simple message: "Distilled, Yet Never Reduced" got the message across that, yes, the BMW 1 was a little matchbox sized car, but it also was just a *distilled* version of its bigger brothers and sisters and was in no way *reduced*. It was still an "ultimate driving machine."

Redlining should accomplish the same thing. We are not reducing the play through the process of redlining, but rather distilling its essence.

If you're making Kentucky bourbon or Scotch whisky, you're *really* in the distillation business. Distillation, according to Wikipedia, "is the process of separating the components or substances from a liquid mixture by using selective boiling and condensation." We've all seen pictures of stills. There's a big vat of alcoholic brew that is heated and run through an intricate, twisting and turning tubing until finally, at the very end of the line, there's a drip, drip, drip of the essence—the whiskey or scotch or brandy.

A director is also in the distillation business. The director's process is also one of separating the components or substances, in this case the parts and elements of the play. Our "boiling" process is one of reading and re-reading, thinking and rethinking, rehearsing and performing. And in the same way, we are condensing the dramatic mixture of information into a theatrical form that will be presented to designers, actors and, ultimately, to an audience.

By redlining your script, you understand its very essence—its distilled core, the sweet spots of its dramatic power. After you complete the process, you should be able to read just the lines that are underlined in red and have a basic understanding of the play in terms of plot, character and emotion.

So, what do you redline? You would redline exposition; you would redline foreshadowing; you would redline dialogue that reveals character objectives; you would redline lines that highlight the themes of the play. You would redline anything that presents the basic plot action in the form of dialogue or stage direction. Whatever is essential that the audience should *see* or *hear* should be redlined. Whatever you don't want them to miss, redline it. Whatever they need to know in order to stay with the play, redline it. "Will you marry me?" "I want a divorce." "He takes the magic potion from a small vial and drinks it, transforming into a donkey." "She spins the dial on the safe, there is a click, and the safe opens."

This can especially help you in your staging. Because we now know that whatever has been redlined must be seen and/or heard by the audience. We can't have the actor in a downstage position, facing upstage, reciting these all-important lines of dialogue that we have underlined in red. We can't have that key bit of stage action, as revealed in the redlined stage directions, missed by the audience because of a supporting character's distracting cross.

Redlining is like an X-ray. It reveals the innermost structure of a play and is an essential directorial technique. Redlining helps to create a powerful and dynamic prompt book and assists a director in making sure that the most important elements of the play receive proper focus and emphasis.

Here's the test. Open the play and read only the lines you've underlined in red. Is the play there? Do you get a distilled version of the play? Have you captured, in the redlines, the essence of the play? If so, you've redlined well. And now you know what absolutely, positively needs attention and emphasis.

CHAPTER 5

Director's Units

An author doesn't write the novel, but writes the chapter, the paragraph, the sentence, the word. The wood worker doesn't make the chair, but the legs, the seat, the back—and then the chair. The painter works in single brush strokes, the choreographer in the smallest of movements.

So too with the play director. You cannot direct the play; you must direct the parts of the play. You cannot direct the whole; you must direct the fragments of the play that make up the whole. And what are these parts? They are not the playwright's scenes; they are the director's units.

When you see the chair, the Chippendale or Hepplewhite or Sheridan, what do you see? You see the chair of course. But if you look closer you realize that the chair is made of different parts, put together—the legs, the back, the seat. It's a structured construction, an assembled creation. What we tend to appreciate is its existence as a unified whole. We don't pay too much attention to the pieces and parts or the seams and spaces between those pieces and parts.

That's the same with a play in production. What the audience experiences is the whole play. Some audience members, those with more watchful eyes, may consciously perceive the more obvious scene by scene construction and progression of events. Fewer still will track the even smaller elements of action, the director's units, the psychological character beats—or recognize as directorial choices the clever blackout or subtle scene-shifting sound cue.

A director, however, must perceive more than the whole or the sum of the parts. The director must identify the smallest directable sections that comprise the play. These units are the very parts that must be joined together, like an elaborate jigsaw puzzle or that Chippendale chair, so that the wholeness of the play will come together and be perceived.

The way to do that is to make decisions that produce manageable and *directable* units.

What are these director's units? They are units of *action*. They are not actor's beats. They are not psychological; they are narrative, and they are plot based. They are events. Your director's units must not be merely descriptive;

they must be defined in such a way that you can actually direct them—and they must lend themselves to the invention of doable action.

How should we define an event onstage? And how can we know the event is over and a new one has begun?

One of the first steps is to title them appropriately and theatrically. The title should not be a verb, but rather a noun. When the event shifts and changes, we have entered into a new director's unit, and the new event needs and deserves its own, new title.

Here are some titles of director's units.

An Argument. A Confession. A Betrayal.
A Murder. A Seduction. A Theft.

A man and a woman are talking in a living room. (A Conversation? A Debate? A Disagreement?). In a play this event could go on for a page or two, or it could take up ten pages of dialogue. The doorbell rings, a man is at the door. (An Interruption? A Delivery? A Burglary?). Now, this event is definitely not the Conversation, Debate or Disagreement that preceded it. It is different and it is new. Therefore, it's a new director's unit.

Directors should strive to define and title these units as precisely as possible, searching always for the most dramatic and theatrical of definitions supported by the action of the play. A Conversation is not as dramatic and theatrical as a Confrontation. A Discussion is not as interesting or as attention-grabbing as an Argument. Look to title the units in ways that define the event onstage truthfully but also in ways that bring out their full dramatic potential.

The entrance or exit of a character almost always signals a new director's unit. The original model for this would be the neoclassical French theatre of Moliere and Racine. With the entrance or exit of any character we have a new scene, sometimes as short as two lines of dialogue. As soon as a new character comes on the stage, we have a new scene. And these scenes are indicated in the script by numbers and the names of the characters.

An example of a French Scene from Molière's *The Miser*:

ACT I.

SCENE I.——VALÈRE, ÉLISE.

Valère. What, dear Élise! You seem so sad after having given me such sweet souvenirs of your love; and I see you sigh when I am full of joy! Can you be so upset that you have made me happy? And do you regret of the engagement my love has forced on you?

Élise. No, Valère, I do not regret anything I have done; I feel compelled by this enchanting power, and I do not desire those things should be any different than they are. But honestly, I am very worried about what may happen; and I fully fear that I love you beyond all measure.

SCENE II.——CLÉANTE, ÉLISE.

Cleante. I am so happy to find you alone. I must speak to you and to tell you a secret, sister.

Élise. I am eager to hear it, brother. Of what is it that you have to say?

Cleante. So many things, sister, but, simply—in one word—love.

After the process of dividing the script into director's units is complete, the next step is to create a plot outline of the play that is based on these units. This is essential as it reveals the play's true narrative structure and extracts and captures the very essence of the play's action. Even with a play that unfolds in a nonlinear manner, each unit consists of action that can be defined in terms of on-stage event.

For the plot outline we will simply write a one or two sentence description of each of our director's units. This provides us with a detailed and concise rendering of the play's plot—it's indispensable and elemental action line.

(See the Plot Outline for our model one-act *Four One-Hundredths* in Chapter 11 for a detailed example.)

Once this is done, and combined with our redlining technique, we should know with accuracy the true story that must be told, the one that is based on the facts of the plot and the actual onstage occurrences that create the narrative. Armed with this powerful information we are now ready to stage the play and to truthfully tell its story.

CHAPTER 6

Color Coding

Color coding is a technique that brings your prompt book alive in a more evocative and theatrical way. It provides a visual dynamic to the director's prompt book that wakes up the script and, in turn, wakes up the director. It goes beyond the notion of merely highlighting a script; it is much more deliberate and specific, more precise and definite.

When we color code, we are reminded of all of the significant visual and aural events of the play. Color coding forces us not to forget what is happening on the page and, more importantly, not to forget what, correspondingly, should be happening on the stage. When we color code, we are nudged and prodded to remember and attend to what the playwright has written and what we have determined should be present in the play's staging. The color-coding process telegraphs that information back to us in a highly effective and vivid way. It is both a reminder and a reinforcer of meaningful information and content.

Without color coding it is easy to forget. It is easy to become immune to the information of the text through the sheer repetition of rehearsal. What color coding provides is a check on what we already know about the play. It is a technique that allows us to maintain the content of the script and make sure that it is transferred to the stage.

Color coding, in essence, is finding information in the script and highlighting it in a way that makes it difficult, if not impossible, to ignore.

We've already learned the technique of redlining. That is the first and primary element of color coding. We have redlined the important lines of dialogue and stage directions as the first way to distill the essential information contained in the script, especially as related to plot, character and emotion.

Now, we are going to account for the other main theatrical ingredients of the text:

THE SOUNDS/THE MUSIC of the play.

> This includes all the sounds, exclusive of spoken dialogue, of the play—from a "sigh" to a clap of thunder.
> and

THE SIGHTS/THE SPECTACLE of the play.

Which will be separated into different color coding for:

> SCENIC ELEMENTS—all significant changes in the scenic environment
> PROPERTIES—the objects that occupy the stage space
> LIGHTING CUES AND EFFECTS—the visual elements provided through lighting design, including projection imagery
> COSTUME ELEMENTS—the important visuals related to clothing, hair and makeup
> PHYSICAL MOVEMENT—the added elements of physicality exclusive of blocking, and any significant additional physical action, such as a slap or a pirouette

The way this works is that we underline in colored pencil any mention of one of these visual or aural elements that appear in the script. We would also include any elements that we, as directors, choose to add that are not included by the playwright. We use a unique color for each element so that each element has its own specific visual identity in the prompt book. In this way they stand out and are made known to the director every time they appear.

This also becomes an effective shortcut when having any conversations or design meetings with individual designers. For example, you can quickly locate all of your prop references and locations in the play simply by scanning the script looking for the coded color for props.

A director may personalize or customize the colors as she or he desires, but here is a suggested color template for the work:

IMPORTANT LINES OF DIALOGUE AND STAGE DIRECTION in **RED** PENCIL
SOUND/MUSIC elements, including Sound Cues in **ORANGE** PENCIL
LIGHTING CUES AND EFFECTS in **BLUE** PENCIL
SCENIC CUES in **GREEN** PENCIL
PROPERTIES in **VIOLET** PENCIL
COSTUMES in **YELLOW** PENCIL
PHYSICAL MOVEMENT in **BROWN** PENCIL

We not only do this on the right-hand page of the prompt book, on the actual words provided by the playwright, but we also reference the same color coding on the left-hand page of the prompt book, in the third of the three columns. This double-coding connects and unites the left- and right-hand pages and unites the words of the playwright with the *vision* of the director. Although this may seem, at first glance, redundant, it actually creates a synergy between the words of the playwright on the right-hand page of the prompt book, and the director's vision that exists on the left-hand page of the book.

Here is a visual example of a left-hand page from a prompt book. This would be opposite the words of the playwright in the script.

Figure 6.1 Left-hand page example.

POINT OF ATTACK: William is active for the 1st time	DIRECTOR'S UNIT 4 TITLE: A CONFESSION PURPOSE: TO EXPOSE W'S INFIDELITY; TO SHOW J'S INTEGRITY	SOUND: TV NEWS BROADCAST
GUN ON WALL: FORESHADOWING OF ACT 3 CLIMAX	W TO GET J to forgive him by telling her the truth CHAR ADJECTIVE/ADVERB: tearfully, remorsefully	REMOTE CONTROL GUN
"Jane was like a force of nature — as fire and earth" → New York Times (possible improv exercise)	J to force W to leave the apartment by screaming at him and breaking plates ADJ/ADV: wildly, angrily	PLATES BREAK
sanc·ti·mo·ni·os → making an exaggerated show of holiness or moral superiority (disapproving)	MOOD: tense, confrontational	DRESS TORN LIGHT FADE
	DIRECTOR'S UNIT 5 TITLE: RECONCILIATION PURPOSE: TO FOCUS ON THE THEME OF FORGIVENESS; TO SHOW J'S STRENGTH	RAIN SFX
Play up the Mood and Atmosphere: cold, rainy night	J TO GET W to stop crying by offering comfort. (HOLDING HER HAND) ADJ/ADV: STRONGLY MOOD: soft, quiet	JANE ON KNEES @ S.R. of SOFA (w/ William's head in lap?) BLACK OUT

CHAPTER 7

The Three Column Left-Hand Page

As Julius Caesar said to his troops, "Divide et impera." Divide and Conquer.

We're not going to war with the script, as the analogy of Caesar's military and political strategy might imply, but we are going to divide the play into three separate directorial arenas in order to gain mastery of it.

We'll first investigate the structure and meaning of the play and then organize our analysis into three specific areas of concern. These areas also happen to represent the three main ways an audience perceives the play. They are the Intellectual, the Emotional and the Sensory. We're going to create, inside the prompt book, on the left-hand page of our book, opposite the playwright's text, three columns in which we will place and hold our analysis, our interpretation and our vision of the play.

The left column, column number one, is the *HEAD* column and will contain our intellectual understanding of the play. It will be our running critical commentary. Any interesting quotes that pertain to the play will go here. Any snippets from reviews of previous productions will go here. Any literary criticism that is pertinent to the play will go here. If there are words that need definitions or instructions on pronunciation, that's column one content. Any of our thinking about the subject or thought of the play will go here as well as any literary analysis and interpretation. So, information about exposition, foreshadowing and thematic statements will all be placed in the left column one. All of the comments on period or style, any research at all, will be placed here. If we are working with a dramaturg, this column would be the place for that pertinent information.

The beauty of this approach is that we are going to put the information in the proper column on the left-hand page of the prompt book *directly across from what it is referencing in the script* on the right-hand page of the prompt book. In this way, when we are rehearsing the second scene in the second act, we have that critical comment from the *New York Times*

DOI: 10.4324/9781003016946-7

about that very scene at our fingertips. That archaic word's definition? It's right there in column one—opposite to where the word appears in the playwright's text.

Some directors may bristle or resist including information from other productions, literary criticism or critics' reviews of the play, but this seems naïve and poorly reasoned. We can and should learn from the intelligent minds, other than our own, who have thoughtfully considered the play. It is really no different than taking in and considering the ideas of our production's collaborators—our designers, our actors, our producers, our artistic directors. Important plays with long histories, plays by major playwrights, plays that have had a considerable amount of production, have also produced a significant amount of critical commentary. There have been thousands of books written about the plays of Shakespeare, Ibsen and Williams. Even a quick Google search of a relatively new play will most likely result in ample production information and a slew of critical reviews. To not consider this information is to direct from a position of both arrogance and ignorance.

The left-hand page's middle column, column number two, is the HEART and GUT column, and it will contain all of the emotional information related to the characters and will give us a language to use with the actors.

Column two is the spine—the vital center—of the left-hand page. It is command central—where we are defining—and titling—the *Director's Units*, where we are accounting for the unit's *Purpose*, and, most importantly, where we are monitoring the *Character Objectives*. We are also using this column to make note of the unit's inherent *Mood* value. There is a lot going on in this column!

Column three, the one on the right, and the one closest to the playwright's text, is the EYE and EAR column. This is the column that breaks down what the audience SEES and what the audience HEARS. It deals with the spectacle and the music of the play. In this column we may have notes on the scenery, the costumes, the lighting—anything the eye can see. Also, we will have notes on the sounds of the play, special effects, music—anything the ear can hear. We may also have diagrams of movement patterns and sketches of the ground plan.

Constructing your prompt book doesn't all happen at once. Each time we read the script, we might add something new, something fresh. Even after we've begun rehearsal with the actors, the prompt book will evolve and change. It's really a living and breathing entity of its own. Tiny adjustments, little improvements on understanding, are made on an ongoing basis; every time you get an idea, it has a place to go. And, always, directly opposite where it belongs—as a directorial response to the playwright's play.

FIRST STEPS

On the left-hand page, make sure the page is divided into three vertically running columns. They can be of roughly the same width, although you may want to make column number two, the middle column, slightly wider in order to contain its content. If you think you have more information in column one, the one on the left, feel free to expand the width of that column instead.

This is important: Before you begin to fill in your three columns, make sure you have first divided the script into the appropriate **Director's Units** with a horizontal line drawn across both the left- and the right-hand pages. Make sure to number your units. See Chapter 5 for more detailed instructions.

These director's units are key to unlocking the play's structure, and they form the basis for many directorial decisions. Base your divisions on shifts of *event* as they occur onstage.

Start to fill in the left column with any pertinent information: Your running critical commentary, your notes on subject and theme. Add the definitions of any words that need defining, any pronunciation keys. Add any quotes from reviews of previous productions. Any notes on period or style.

In the center column, number and give each director's unit a definitive **Title** that describes what happens in that unit. Think of the *noun* that defines the event. For example, A Confession, A Proposal, An Arrest, etc.

Under the title, write the **Purpose** of each director's unit. It could be "to introduce the subject and theme of vengeance" or "to provide exposition about the death of Hamlet's father" or "to build suspense." This will be the main effect we will want to achieve; it will be a directorial goal for the unit.

Define the inherent **Mood** in each unit. Is it "dark and dreary" or "bright and cheery"? Is it "upbeat, and sparkly like a gemstone" or "slow and sad as a mourner"?

In the center column, column two, list each character in the action unit, their **Objectives** and character **Adjectives and Adverbs**.

Provide character objectives that focus on an observable change in the other person. Direct the action outward toward a shift in behavior or attitude in the other. "To force X to leave the room." "To make Y look at me."

Add a phrase that indicates "how" the character objective is being accomplished. "To force X to leave the room *by threatening to call the police, by raising my voice, by stomping my feet*."

Add character adjectives and/or adverbs that modify the objective by qualifying the "how." "*Calmly*," "*Hysterically*," "*Quietly*," etc.

Example: To force Xavier to leave the room by threatening to call security. (Calmly and quietly.)

The actors will come with their own understanding and intentions for the characters, their own agency for creating the roles. By doing your analysis and interpretation of the script, however, and by taking a direct role in analyzing *all* of the play's characters and their motivations, you can better coach and guide the entire cast. The result will be more unity in the total communication of the play through character.

You may even write multiple and different objectives, thinking of them as potential possibilities or ways an actor may address their character's intent in the particular director's unit. The same is true for your character adjectives and adverbs; you can write alternative ways to accomplish the same objective. Then you can work through these alternatives—with the actor—in rehearsal, testing for which may be the best approach to create the most powerful, truthful and theatrical character objectives and actions for the unit.

Fill in column three with the appropriate information regarding music and spectacle.

As stated earlier, feel free to choose your own colors. Just make sure you maintain the consistency of the color coding.

Here is a suggested color palate:

IMPORTANT LINES OF DIALOGUE OR STAGE DIRECTION in **RED** PENCIL.
SOUND CUES in **ORANGE** PENCIL
LIGHT CUES in **BLUE** PENCIL
SCENIC CUES in **GREEN** PENCIL
PROPERTIES in **VIOLET** PENCIL
COSTUMES in **YELLOW** PENCIL
PHYSICAL ACTION in **BROWN** PENCIL

You may be wondering where you put your notes on blocking. Your preliminary or paper blocking will be placed not the left-hand page but on the right-hand dialogue page. The blocking notation will be put right on the word of dialogue or the word of stage directions where it occurs. You may want to sketch out some diagrams of more intricate movement work in column three, but place the blocking on the right-hand page. More on that in the next chapter.

CHAPTER 8

The Right-Hand Page

As Shakespeare wrote, "the play's the thing," and the right-hand pages of the prompt book are mainly the domain of the playwright. These are the pages that contain the words written by the playwright. But the right-hand page is also where the director will notate the blocking, place references to the technical cues, and draw horizontal lines to delineate the director's units of action.

Importantly, this is also where we have our redlining and some of the color coding we learned about in Chapters 4 and 7.

In one sense, this is the easiest page because so much is already given—the lines of dialogue and stage directions as written by the playwright. We may choose to think of the stage directions as "suggestions" rather than as requirements, but they need to be fully analyzed and considered. Even the way the playwright has placed the words on the page needs our attention. Is a word *italicized*? Is there a period, an exclamation point or a question mark at the end of the line? <u>Is a word or a line of dialogue underlined</u>? Do we have a three-dot ellipsis to … ponder the meaning of? Or a dash at the end of a line—OR IS A WORD OR SENTENCE IN ALL CAPS. And then … what if part of a line of dialogue is <u>*IN ALL CAPS AND ALSO ITALICIZED AND UNDERLINED*</u>? These are clues and cues, subtle—and not so subtle—suggestions and keys as to how lines should be delivered. Sometimes playwrights have very unique and individual ways of expressing themselves on the page. Suzan-Lori Parks, for example, uses forward slashes (//) to indicate overlapped dialogue. One of the main things these graphical idiosyncrasies do is create the rhythm of the lines—which is why the playwright has employed them. It's a way for the playwright to code the script, to leave us some bread crumbs, some extra information that will lead to their intended interpretation. Many playwrights will provide a key at the beginning of a script to help you "decode" their signals.

They also help us understand proper emphasis—what should be stressed and what should not. They lead us to understand what the playwright has "heard" in her head that needs some special attention when an actor speaks the line. We often have to read the play several times before this coding becomes clear and evident.

There may be "beats" or "pauses" written into the play by the playwright. There may be long stretches of white space with no lines at all. These are all parts of what needs to be considered in the process of directing the play. How the playwright lays the words on the page can be a major part of their artistry and a necessary element that needs to be interpreted and controlled for in performance.

When we divide the script into director's units, we draw a horizontal line across both the left-hand page and the right-hand page. This creates a clear and decisive division between one unit and another, one dramatic event and another. Just as it divides one unit from another, it also visually creates a strong linkage that interconnects and unites the director's left-hand page with the mostly playwright's right-hand page.

Specific blocking notation is best placed on the right-hand page directly off the line of dialogue or stage direction to which it applies. Use the left and/or right margins or any available white space to place your blocking notation. Use an abbreviated, short-hand system because, in a script, empty white space to make notes is usually at a premium. Use X for Cross, USL for Upstage Left, etc. Make sure you use a pencil. Blocking has a way of always changing. Each director should feel free to create their own system of notation, e.g., a circle with a C in it for costumes, a circle with an L in it for lights.

The right-hand page should also be the place where technical cues are recorded. Some will be evident on a first-read of the script, others will be developed in the rehearsal process, and some will not be identified until the technical rehearsal process begins, and in conjunction with the stage manager and designers. They will be notated by number and letter. Place them in the right margin of the right-hand page, and make sure that you number or label them during the technical rehearsal process. In this way you can quickly and easily work with your stage manager when any issue related to calling the cues for the show comes up. You will always know where the cues are and what their proper call numbers or letters are.

CHAPTER 9

Using the Prompt Book to Schedule and Organize for Artistic Success

The American author, businessman and time management guru, Stephen Covey, said that "the key is not to prioritize what's on your schedule, but to schedule your priorities." By creating your prompt book, you have identified the significant and vital needs, the artistic demands, of the play, and now, armed with this knowledge, you can schedule an effective rehearsal process to accomplish your goals.

It is the very work you've done on your prompt book that will guide you and inform you on just how to schedule your rehearsals.

The great Canadian hockey legend, Wayne Gretzky said, "I don't skate to where the puck is, but to where the puck will be." This is exactly what a director must do. You have to skate to opening night even when you are only at the first read through. A good rehearsal schedule sharpens your skates, points you in the right direction—and, if all goes well, gets you where you need to be by the time the play opens.

The two images of the compass and the map are great emblems for the director. The map is the play; the compass is our directing vision and skill. We are constantly trying to move toward that true north—that which is the fullest realization of the play we are directing.

In the theatre the rehearsal and production schedules are the scaffolding that structures the work, and they defend us from chaos. It is the director who mainly sets and defines the rehearsal schedule. Of course, there will be consultation with the producer and other production departments, especially for the scheduling of the technical and dress rehearsals, but to develop the play's rehearsal schedule is one of the director's primary responsibilities and a necessary talent to be developed.

The quality of rehearsal determines the quality of performance, and it follows that the quality of the rehearsal schedule itself will have a huge impact hours to a dialect coach? Is it an original play, and is the playwright doing rewrites? Is the cast made up of highly professional and experienced actors or are they a group of first-time amateurs? Is there stage combat? Do you have two weeks of rehearsal or eight weeks of rehearsal? Are you working on an Equity contract schedule or are you rehearsing at school after a full day of classes? There are so many possible variables; this is why there are no hard and fast rules to employ when designing a rehearsal schedule. Each play is unique, with its own set of very specific demands, and it is the director's job to evaluate and consider all of them. All of these many factors will contribute to how the rehearsal schedule is constructed.

It is the early work, however, that you have done on your prompt book and your understanding of the strengths and weaknesses of your creative team that will guide you in creating an effective and dynamic schedule.

At the beginning of the process remember that you are not rehearsing the play, but the parts of the play.

There are some standard and traditional formulas that have served directors well, and rehearsals can be broken down into certain specific areas.

They are:

TABLE WORK
STAGING REHEARSALS

> Blocking
> Review
> Run

WORK REHEARSALS (for Character Development and Enhancement/Enrichment)
TECHNICAL AND DRESS REHEARSALS
and
PICK UP REHEARSALS AFTER OPENING

By closely considering your prompt book you can assess how much time is needed for each of these basic rehearsal areas. In truth, these areas often overlap and interplay with each other. Table work, for example, never truly ends. We're forever reading the play and revaluating the written word, finding new elements, new meanings and new nuances that need attention. Staging may continue to evolve even through dress rehearsals, especially if required to accommodate a costume change or the timing of a scene shift. Some elements of the technical process may even be introduced in the early stages of rehearsal well before the official technical rehearsals begin. Work rehearsals overlap with Staging Rehearsals. Run throughs occur at various stages and to differing degrees; we might run a scene, an act, or the entire play.

Let's take a look at each of these broader rehearsal areas in turn:

TABLE WORK

Table work usually occupies the first day or more of rehearsal. It is time spent with the script without a need for the actors to be on their feet, on a stage, acting. Some directors and some actors like to spend lots of time at the table, discussing and analyzing the script, talking about the period, investigating the subject matter and themes of the play and breaking down the character beats. Other directors and other actors prefer to dispense with these types of rehearsals as quickly as possible and get up on their feet and start moving the play. Each play may require its own schedule in terms of table work. As the director you lead the way on how much time you and your company of actors and designers will devote to this stage of the process. It's basically the more academic and intellectual part of the rehearsal process. It's also the time when you, as the director, will introduce the play to the cast. You can describe why you chose the play, what drew you to the subject matter, how the themes resonate with you and why you think it is a worthy choice for presentation to your audience.

The table work rehearsals also are an especially good time to reinforce the narrative of the play, to share with the cast your understanding of its structure, to start the process of defining the identities and relationships of the characters, to explore the impact of the subject and theme of the play as revealed through its action, and to clarify the style and scheme of production that you will employ.

Often it is helpful to use this time, when the actors have their scripts on the table, to share the director's units that you have established in your prompt book. I like to have the actors draw horizontal lines across their scripts to denote the beginning and end of each director's unit. This is a vivid and graphic technique that helps remind and reinforce, in a subtle but powerful way, the very structure of the play as you have determined it to be, and this understanding of the play's dramatic structure is strengthened every time the actor picks up the script. It is also valuable because these director's units will be used to call actors to rehearsal. This information about the director's units will also be available to the actors in the plot outline that you give them.

You can use the table work to help the actors understand what they need to do to realize the play and what they must communicate to an audience. All plays are communications and the actor is the direct link to the audience in the communication process. A prime obligation of the actor is to communicate plot, and they do this through their communication of character, specifically through the actions of the character. Table work is an opportunity for the director to talk about this link between the actions of the characters and the expression of the play's plot.

Since plot is so key, a crucial responsibility of the actors is to simply tell the story of the play. I always like to share with the actors my plot outline of the play which specifies each and every directorial unit's narrative contribution to telling the play's story. See an example of a plot outline in the chapter devoted to our model one-act, *Four One-Hundredths*.

It is also common practice to include designer presentations in these first rehearsals so the actors can better understand the physical world within which they will be performing. This is an opportunity not only for the designers to personally engage and share their creativity with the actors but also for you to reinforce the larger sense of collaboration at work in the production. The designers are equal contributors to the artistic expression, and their work needs to be honored and incorporated accordingly. Your design notes, which have been placed in your prompt book, can be used at this time to facilitate the conversation about the design of the play with the company.

One of the prime objectives of this first phase of the rehearsal process is to create ensemble—to bring the actors together as collaborators sharing in an artistic journey. It's about getting everyone on the same page—helping everyone associated with the play to understand its meanings, its significance, its values. Creating a rehearsal environment conducive to creativity and collaborative exploration is a major goal in these first few rehearsals. Some directors may use ensemble building exercises, improvisations, or trust games to achieve this. Sometimes simple movement and vocal warm-ups can serve the purpose. If the actors are part of a conservatory program, they may have already spent several hours in voice, speech and movement classes, and will not need an extensive warm-up routine prior to beginning rehearsals. Other casts may need a more thorough warm-up to prepare to rehearse.

Everyone will begin by the end of the first week to have a clearer comprehension of the basic elements of the play and a stronger understanding of the action line that communicates the story. You have discovered much of this in your initial prompt book process. As this first rehearsal period progresses, characterizations will be in their infancy, but will start to emerge with a sharper sense of direction. This is a time for you to engender in the cast your passion for the play.

A sense of the theatre discipline needed to create a quality performance will be understood by the actors as you, the director, model professionalism and commitment to the project. The early form of how the rehearsals will be conducted begins to be known. Do you start exactly on time? Do the stage managers have everything organized before rehearsals begin? Is the stage floor taped with the ground plan of the play for the first day of blocking?

You may choose to offer more formal, written guidelines for rehearsal. I recommend this. Even professional Equity actors have official rules of "Actors' Etiquette." Once it's in writing, it is known. It becomes the expected way to behave. It becomes your standard operating procedure and your protocol for success. "Arrive on time. Always have your script available. Bring a pencil, not a pen, to rehearsal. No food backstage. Turn off all cell phones. Be supportive of other cast members. Contact the Stage Manager if you are going to be late." Each director may have their own ideas about what to offer the actors. Some may call them rules; some may call them guidelines. It helps to clarify expectations, and it is important to do so as soon as the rehearsals begin. A copy of your guidelines can be placed in your prompt book for reference.

STAGING REHEARSALS

Staging rehearsals are used to establish the basic pattern of movement for the play. Some directors have very specific visions of how a play may present itself visually through physical movement and come to these rehearsals with a very detailed and precise sense of staging. Other directors will work with and through the actors in an improvisational way to discover and find the basic movement structure of the play.

If you are well-schooled in the fundamentals of stage directing and the underlying principles of movement, you will probably have some very definite ideas about what will work and what will not work in terms of staging. Usually for a director in the early stage of their career it is always a good idea to have some preliminary decisions made regarding the play's blocking, especially in regards to the beginnings and endings of scenes and the entrances and exits of characters. This saves precious rehearsal time. It also builds confidence in the actors that the director knows their way around a stage and set.

If you've redlined your script, you already know what the emphatic lines of dialogue are and what are the most important lines of stage direction. You will block the play so that these lines receive proper emphasis, so that the audience sees and hears what they need to see and hear. Redlines are often the first key to powerful and effective staging as they indicate what actor needs an advantageous, usually upstage, position in relationship to the other actors in the scene, during delivery of those lines.

Some directors pre-block by making sketches and diagrams of the staging. Other directors may use their designer-provided set model to help visualize the movement. Some directors move toy figures around. Another useful technique is to just close your eyes and visualize the action. This can also be aided by recording a reading of the play and listening and imagining what the movement might be. The main goal is to allow for the story of the play to be told visually and to use movement and all the available visual elements to communicate the story, the characters and the emotion of the play.

Sometimes it is easiest to start building your blocking in your prompt book with what you absolutely know based on the playwright's text. There's a knock on the door and the character enters; that's easy. There is a line of stage direction about putting logs on the fire; that's simple, we're at the fireplace Upstage Left for that moment. Sometimes you may also just have a gut feeling that that one moment in the second act should take place Downstage Right in a spot of blue light. Write it down in column three of your prompt book! And place your blocking in the script on the right-hand page exactly where it occurs.

What you are always looking for, when you're alone with the script, in private or in rehearsal with the actors, is that visual moment, a cross, a light cue, a gesture, that communicates a value in the play.

The preparatory work you have done in your prompt book helps you know what is working in rehearsal and what is not. It is what you check your work against. The prompt book is a compass; it lets you know if you are still on course or heading in the wrong direction. Combined with the new discoveries made in rehearsal and the collaborative contributions of the actors and designers, you are now in a better position to shape the visual expression of the play on stage. Your three-column prompt book has prepared you to more fully and confidently understand the value of what is now occurring in rehearsal and how to judge the quality of the work being done. The prompt book has become both a catalyst and a facilitator of creativity and a springboard for success in rehearsal. Things may change and new revelations made, but the prompt book is there as a monitor and as a reminder of your initial intent.

With staging you start with the overview, the larger, more general pattern of movement. You handle the larger bits of business—the opening of the important letter, the mixing of the poison potion, the on-bended-knee proposal of marriage, the drawing of swords. Then we find the smaller more nuanced pieces of movement and smaller bits of business that fill in-between and connect to these larger moments—the small sideways look, the telling gesture, the movement of the window shade in the breeze.

It's a little bit like a child's connect-the-dots drawing. There are the big dots that define the larger elements of the picture, and then there are the smaller dots that fill in and complete the whole. The first task is to define those big dot moments and how they should look and how they should *move*.

Then we start to figure out how we get from big moment to big moment. What are the little steps in-between? As with the play itself we are not blocking the whole play in one fell swoop. We are going one step at a time, beat by beat, line by line, scene by scene, act by act.

Move around the theatre to see how your staging is working from various locations in the house. Check the sightlines. Walk the back row from side to side to see if the blocking is working from all audience angles.

This first phase of the staging or blocking rehearsals leaves us with a rough draft of the play's movement structure. Some scenes may be more developed than others, closer to a finished product, and other scenes may just be sketched-in, still needing further development. At this stage we should start to see the outlines of the whole, the rough, but still incomplete, staging of the entire play. At this point the actors probably still have their scripts in hand so the staging is, by its very nature, unfinished.

As we return to review the units that have been staged, we can start to add detail and nuance to each unit. We can now begin to finish and polish it. This is also when we can begin to work toward a more refined sense of character development.

Repetition results in retention. As you review and repeat scenes and units of action, the actors start to retain the blocking, they start to refine their line readings, and the play itself starts to come into sharper focus.

I cannot stress enough the importance of review and repetition for both the actors and the director. By the actors doing it multiple times, they learn the blocking. By seeing it multiple times, the director understands its quality and value. Is that cross necessary? Is that blocking pattern awkward? Does it make sense that the actor sits on *that* line, or should she sit on the one *before*? You can only truly evaluate the quality of the staging by having it repeated several times.

One of the most effective ways to determine the best blocking is to repeat a sequence multiple times in *different* ways and see what looks best to you and feels best for the actors. Often it can be a choice of just three options. For example, should the actor cross *before* the line, *after* the line, or *on* the line? Should she sit *before* the line, *after* the line, or *on* the line? Usually, one of these three possibilities is the better option. Each variation has a slightly different meaning. The emphasis and interpretation of the lines change depending on how they correlate with the movement. You can test it by sampling the options, and then, together with the actor, find out what works best. Usually, emphasis falls on whatever is last in the sequence. Say the line and then point—the pointing receiving focus. Sit and then say the line—the line of dialogue receives emphasis. Sitting and saying the line at the same time or pointing and saying the line at the same time—the emphasis is equal.

It's also important to communicate the message that these are rehearsals and not performances. Take the pressure off the actors to "perform." Let them experiment. Let them find their way without always looking for results. Let them *rehearse*.

The basic structure of the Staging Rehearsals can be thought of in three distinct phases:

BLOCKING REHEARSALS
REVIEW REHEARSALS
RUN REHEARSALS

In the blocking phase we are looking to set the rough pattern of movement. This is where the power of column three—the Eye and Ear column—of your prompt book comes into play. As we begin to focus on the physical and aural expression of the play, we use our prompt book to guide us. Column three also becomes a check against our original ideas related to how the play presents itself visually and aurally.

Our paper blocking is easily and quickly available to us on the prompt book's right-hand page—directly and appropriately scored next to the playwright's lines. We may also have additional movement sketches available to us as placed in column three of the left-hand page.

Make sure your stage managers are keeping an accurate record in their prompt books, and make sure the actors are writing down their blocking. In pencil. One with an eraser on the end. Blocking rarely stays the same the first time it is done. Changes will occur.

Have a triple record of the blocking: In your prompt book, in the stage manager's prompt book and in the actors' scripts. Nothing is more frustrating than to have had a productive blocking rehearsal on Monday only to return on Tuesday and no one remembers the brilliant blocking that was created the day before.

In the Review Rehearsal phase, we are simply reviewing what we've done the day before. It is vitally important to *always* review the blocking work of the previous day to reinforce it and to get a running start on the next unit of action. Calling the rehearsals by the director's unit numbers, as developed in your prompt book, reinforces the internal, dramaturgical structure of the play, not just on the page, but on the stage. Starting and stopping work at director's unit breaks is an excellent way to strengthen the actors' performances in relation to the play's own dramatic structure. Always start and stop on the unit breaks that you have created in your prompt book. Always go back and begin from the beginning of a director's unit. Always stop at the point where you've completed a director's unit.

Review rehearsals take place during all phases of the rehearsal process, not just in the staging phase. You will always benefit from reviewing the previous day's rehearsal work.

Play close attention to your color coding, especially in column three, to make sure that all of the physical and visual elements of the play, as identified and expressed in your prompt book, have been attended to and are present in your staging.

Once the basic movement is blocked and reviewed for further enrichment, we can move on to the more substantive Work Rehearsals where we will go deeper into the details of each individual unit of action.

WORK REHEARSALS
Enhancement and Enrichment

The Work Rehearsals are primarily devoted to character development and the enhancement and enrichment of all of our ongoing work on the play. This is when you will be leaning heavily on the content you developed in column two of your prompt book—the Heart and Gut column.

At this point it would be advisable to have the actors off book and no longer with scripts in hand. The blocking, if not completely set, is closer to its finished form and should be repeatable with a consistent result.

Now, with the general blocking completed, we can turn to working more closely on the more subtle elements of the script and the invention of detailed action and behavior that will enhance and enrich the play. We are working toward a greater sense of coordinated, ensemble playing by the actors as well as more imaginative and theatrical individual performances. Each potential theatrical detail is looked at directorially for its ability to communicate—each composition, each movement, each line reading, each moment is evaluated. We ask the questions, "What's missing?" "What's needed?" "How can this scene, this speech, this moment better communicate the playwright's words?" We are now more than ever looking at the details.

We are trying to enlarge and intensify the dramatic elements of each moment, sharpen the connection between action and reaction, add variety, and bring increased theatrical energy to the play. We begin, for the first time, to really see the rhythm and tempo pulse through the show. A consistency in performance starts to emerge. There is a unity, there is a sense of flow. Scenes build, moments connect. Something satisfying is occurring. The play is becoming itself; it's about to be born.

Continue to use the material in the middle column to guide the actors in understanding each unit's action, mood and purpose, and in developing their characterizations and physicalizing their roles. Pay special attention to the character objectives as analyzed in column two. Use your prompt book to monitor your progress. The character objectives will influence blocking, and the blocking may, in turn, influence character objectives.

Throughout this phase of the rehearsal process we are trying to bring increased unity to every moment and element of the play by: (1) strengthening the emphasis placed on the significant plot moments, (2) deepening and illuminating character values and (3) enriching the emotional life of the play.

One technique that is often helpful is to take a step back, return to table work and start rehearsing a scene by simply sitting at a table with the actors and reading through it. Literally. From the script. Reading it from the script, taking the eyes of the actors back to the text. This gives us a renewed contact with the playwright's words, lets us know if we've added words or deleted them, missed a written moment of business or a line of stage direction. You'd be surprised at how often we might have missed a "pause" or a "he looks at her askance" or some clue or other small piece of information that the playwright has provided. An actor may have inverted a couple of words, and now that they are placed back in their proper order, the line reads more smoothly and makes more sense.

After reading the scene we have a brief discussion. What have we discovered? What has changed? What new insights have we gained? If nothing else, this technique will boost and help set the accurate memorization of the lines. Then clear the table, put the scripts down and get the actors back on their feet and onstage—and run the scene. This technique, a return to table work, can really reinforce the words of the play on the page and has the ability to translate into deeper work on the stage. It also takes the director back more directly to their prompt book and reconnects the director to all of the preparation work they have done.

The next phase after the Working Rehearsals would be Run Rehearsals. This is when we run without stops or interruptions longer sequences of action, larger groups of directorial units. These Run Rehearsals will develop into full scale run-throughs, first of individual acts and then of the entire play.

Work Rehearsals and Run Rehearsals can sometimes be used in tandem. One might start a rehearsal by working a scene or an act for an hour and then running it. The advantage here is we refine and develop the scene or act and then, by running it, see if that work holds up. We can also reverse the order and start a rehearsal with a run through of a group of scenes or an entire act, and then follow-up with a working rehearsal. In this way we use the run through as a diagnostic to see exactly what sections need work—and then we work those sections.

Some directors find it helpful to actually time their run throughs and to keep a record of the times as a way to better understand the rhythm and tempo of the play.

As we move toward the Technical and Dress Rehearsals it is important that scripts are left offstage, that the memorization of the text and the movement patterns are firmly in place and that the rhythms of the play are beginning to express themselves consistently and with a sense of theatrical grace.

As the director, you will start to see the play gel, to come together. The emotional life of the play will present itself in a more connected way. You will begin to see the play unite as a work of art. Don't neglect to look for any issues or problems that might need corrective measures. Maybe an entrance is poorly timed. Maybe a key plot point is too subtle and requires more emphasis. Maybe a line reading needs punching up. Now is the time to be ruthlessly honest about what is working and what is not and to make adjustments to improve the overall communication of the play. Get it to work onstage not just in your head. What once made sense in your mind might not be working onstage. Now is not the time to debate or intellectualize, but rather to shape physical action. Make it happen onstage. Do it now!

In some ways, as directors, we are moving away from a focus on our written prompt book, and, now, more and more, to the events that are occurring before us onstage. It can still, however, be incredibly helpful for a director to sit down and read through their prompt book at this phase in the rehearsal process. Reestablish contact with the prompt book, read your notes from column one, look at the scene purposes as stated in column two, review the color-coded work in column three. See what may have slipped by you, what might need reinforcing, what detail or nuance may need to be added to lift up a scene or moment.

This enrichment stage in the rehearsal process never really ends. It continues through the last day of performance, but the bulk of the work is done now in this phase of rehearsal. The play is alive and constantly evolving, but a director's attention to the quality of performance continues until the play closes. The play is beginning to call out for the addition of scenery, costumes, lighting, sound—and an audience.

As we move closer to the technical and dress rehearsals, we continue to refine and sharpen the show. We are not making substantial changes or reinterpreting the play in any major way. We don't, however, stop directing. We continue to look for what can be done to enhance and improve the performance. We are looking closely at every moment and making smaller, but important, adjustments and corrections. We are usually not adding major new elements, but we are looking for any additional opportunities to clarify and sharpen the communication of the play.

We are also employing the use of our run-throughs to build momentum for the show. We are focusing more on *when* events occur onstage and for *how long*. Rhythm and tempo become major considerations for the first time. We are focused on pace. My directing teacher, Larry Carra, used to talk about "the race to the curtain" and how we wanted to build energy to bring the play home, to create a satisfying ending for the show.

For these final run throughs, I like to ask the actors to remain backstage. No more sitting in the house. It's close to show time, and I want to send that message. We want to get into a show frame of mind. We run the acts and keep the intermission the same length as it will be when we perform. Do everything as close as possible to the way it will be done when we open—minus the costumes and tech. We want to replicate the performance conditions as much as possible.

One of the other main objectives of these final rehearsals before tech is to create a sense of assurance and belief in everything we have done to this point. The actors have to feel, to sense, to know that they are ready to perform this play. Your notes, which may have been mostly corrective up to this point, should now shift and be used with more affirmative intent to reinforce what the actors are doing right, what's good about their work. They need to know and feel that they are doing a good job. Build them up and prepare them to perform before a live audience through positive notes. Instill confidence.

Make sure you block your curtain call if you will be using one. This also sends a very clear signal to the actors that the show is about to open. You don't want to be stuck in a tech rehearsal with an entire crew watching you figure out the curtain call. It should be rehearsed just like every other scene of the play in the days prior to the first technical rehearsal and incorporated into all of the run-throughs of the show. Are there any special sound or light cues that might accompany the curtain call? Make sure those cues were discussed in the paper tech and incorporated into the stage manager's prompt book.

TECHNICAL AND DRESS REHEARSALS

The technical and dress rehearsal phase of the process is perhaps the most rewarding and exciting of all the rehearsal phases as it is the time when the play comes fully to life and claims its true identity with all of the theatrical elements coming into place: scenery, costumes, lighting, sound. If the previous phase was the pregnancy, this is the period of labor and birth.

For the director, two key themes for the technical and dress rehearsals are *anticipation* and *patience*. As much as possible you want to have anticipated any possible problem areas before the technical rehearsals begin. That's why it is so important to have developed your prompt book; the prompt book gives you clarity about your intention before even the first rehearsal. Ideally, you have used your prompt book as a tool to help guide the designers' interpretations of the play, and you have used your prompt book to record the technical and costume decisions you have made along the way. You've also coordinated your prompt book with the stage manager's prompt book so that all the cues and needed information for a successful technical rehearsal are in their proper places.

It is also important that throughout the time before the tech and dress rehearsals you have had regular and productive production meetings. This is where the anticipation part comes in: You have anticipated what is required for the play, what needs to be done and who needs to do it. You have tested props. You've had design meetings. You've looked at costume sketches. You've browsed through the racks of clothes in the costume shop. You've seen paint samples. You've heard sound cues. All before walking into that first technical rehearsal. The last thing you want is to be surprised at tech about anything. Anticipate. Know in advance as much as you can about where the designers and technicians are in the process, what they need, what their limitations are, what they've already done and what their time requirements are to complete their jobs.

This is why "making the rounds" is so important. It's critical that throughout the entire production period you visit the various departments on a regular basis. Stop by the scene shop, talk to the Tech Director, see the progress they're making on constructing that fireplace. Drop into the costume shop. See the fabric *before* they start cutting and draping it. Have a coffee with the Lighting Designer. Basically, check in with everybody. Be available for questions, clarifications. Carry your prompt book with you in case you need to reference anything in it! Use your prompt book to guide conversations and to find answers to those questions. Use the words of the playwright and the work you've done on the play in your prompt book as evidence and support for your interpretation of the play. Give appreciation and encouragement. Thank people for everything they're doing to help you achieve your vision. They don't work for you, they work with you, and you probably can't do anything close to what they can do in their own individual areas; so, be grateful for the help.

One of the main goals for the director during the technical process is to achieve a unity of production. We are bringing all of the elements together—scenery, props, costumes, lighting, sound—to achieve a common creative objective.

Remember too that, although you are the director, the techs and dresses are not your rehearsals. They are the rehearsals of the designers and crews. You and the actors are there to help and assist them, not the other way around. You may oversee these rehearsals and be a source for certain decision-making, but the agenda for these rehearsals is set by the Technical Director and the design team.

To have a successful tech rehearsal everyone on the production team must have considered the viability and achievability of everything that is going to happen onstage *before* the first day of technical rehearsals. This means we've had our design meetings; we've had our production meetings. Things have been tested, previewed and examined from all possible angles.

To have a productive and successful tech, all of the key elements must be in place and ready to go. That means the walls have to be up—and painted—before the lighting crew can focus the instruments. If we're going to rehearse that quick change, we need that costume and the dresser. We also need that Equity light backstage—and working—so the dresser can better assist the actor with that zipper. Everyone should be helping everyone else do their jobs better.

Remember, that the crews need to rehearse just like the actors needed to rehearse. These are their days. They deserve their time, their practice, their rehearsal. Sometimes you may need to encourage them to do some of these rehearsals "dry," on their own, without the actors. There may be a particularly difficult scene shift that is simply taking too long. You may, as a director, request that they take a look at that tomorrow without the actors present.

If you happen to be working in academic theatre, remember that sometimes you may have a board operator who is doing their first show and has never operated the light or sound board before, except in the lab. Be patient and allow the crew to learn what they need to do to help you realize the show.

In coordination with the Technical Director and design team you will have already developed the tech schedule in advance. Make sure that the major technical elements are given enough time to be worked through so they will be successful. Some technical cues, and you don't always know which cues they will be before you are working on them, will take longer than others. Usually the first half-a-dozen cues in a show take the longest; everybody is just getting started on the show. Some cues need to be rehearsed several times. Others may be handled with a simple note that will be implemented the next day.

Trust that the Stage Manager will keep things moving, but, if they are not, encourage them to take a firmer leadership role in running the technical rehearsals and to get things on track.

Reread your prompt book prior to the first tech. Look at every single cue. Visualize them in your mind. Go over them with your stage manager. Attend the paper tech. Discuss what's going to happen before it happens. Make sure you pay special attention to the most important cues. Prioritize. If you tell your team that this one light cue in scene six is super important to you *before* the tech rehearsal, then when you get to that cue in the theatre, the crew will be prepared and will understand the importance of that cue—and will spend the time getting it right.

Anticipation avoids and solves many potential problems. Test that special prop days before in rehearsal if you can. Make sure it works as you want it to work. In rehearsal with the actors, you can use rehearsal props to prepare them for the real ones, rehearsal costumes to stand-in during that quick change in act three. This will make things go so much smoother when the real items are in place at the technical rehearsal. It won't be the first time an actor has handled a physical object at that moment in the play.

It's also your job as director to prepare the cast for the tech rehearsal. Obviously, that means, at minimum, that they know their lines, they are completely comfortable with their blocking, and that they are absolutely clear on their entrances and exits. Make sure they also understand that these are not rehearsals for them, but are for the designers and the technicians. Remind the actors that these rehearsals are for the crew. The actors are there to help the crew do their jobs better and more easily—which means these rehearsals are also not for the director. Avoid doing anything directorially with the actors. No line notes. No blocking notes—unless you need to make a change because something has come up that requires an adjustment for technical reasons.

The tech and dress rehearsals are great opportunities to have the entire production team together and to finalize the building of the show before an audience enters into the mix. It is an opportunity to create a larger sense of community and a chance for a higher level of collaboration.

Make sure that you—and your actors—give thanks and show appreciation to everyone on the crew that is helping to realize the full potential of the play through their efforts and talent. Show and encourage respect for these contributors and their contributions.

With student actors, in particular, make sure that they have been briefed on what to expect and what they need to be prepared to do. The actors need to be dressed in clothing that approximates the performance costumes, especially in regards to color, so that the lighting designer is seeing something as close as possible to what will appear during dress rehearsals. They need to know the backstage routes for entrances and exits, the locations of the prop tables. They need to be prepared to work in minimal backstage light. They need to know that they must remain available for appearances onstage throughout the entire process—that they need to communicate with the Assistant Stage Manager any trips to the bathroom or emergency phone calls.

Most importantly, they need to know that they must remain quiet backstage and silent onstage while the designers and technicians do their work. Nothing is more frustrating for a tech staff than to have actors talking and moving around onstage while they are trying to set a cue.

Make sure you write down your notes as the tech and dress rehearsals are going on. Give notes to your designers and department heads. Talk with them at the start of the next technical or dress rehearsal, with your notes in hand, to check on the progress from yesterday's rehearsal and ask if there are any questions. Always have your prompt book with you for reference.

It's traditional for directors to give out opening night cards or gifts. If you plan on doing that, and I recommend it, it might be a good idea to get started on those sooner rather than later, especially if you have a large cast. If you give gifts, they don't have to be expensive, but a small token of appreciation is another way to say thank you to cast and crew. A card with a personal note is actually probably more meaningful.

PICK UP REHEARSALS

When there may be several days between performances, the director may often want to call for pick up rehearsals. This is especially true in non-professional or academic theatre. These pick up rehearsals are used to keep the show fresh and ensure that the actors are ready to perform again. If you're directing a musical, a physical theatre piece or a play with stage combat, it's always a good idea to call for pick up rehearsals. In the case of plays involving stage combat, you will want to have daily calls prior to performance. Some dance numbers may also require pick up rehearsals prior to every performance. Sometimes these can also be used as a type of company warm-up.

As the creator of the rehearsal schedule, the director must learn to assess how much time will be needed to rehearse each part or section of the play. Each play will have its own needs and its own timetable. Generally, you can think that you will need at least an hour for every minute of stage time. A two-hour show will need 120 hours of rehearsal at minimum. If you are working an Equity schedule of 6 ½ hours a day with 90 minutes of breaks, six days a week, that's a three-week rehearsal period. If you're only rehearsing three or four hours a day, five days a week, that's more like five or six weeks of rehearsal. Some plays will require more time, some less, depending on many different factors. Are you working with professional actors or amateurs? Do you have musical numbers and a large cast or are you working with a small ensemble of three actors in a straight play? Can the producers afford an additional week of rehearsal? Experience will guide you. At the beginning of your career, plan for more time than you may need; you can always cancel or shorten rehearsals, or give people a day off. You can't create an eighth day in a week.

Directors set the table and lead the way. It's important to understand that it is the director, more than anyone else, who creates the artistic environment, sets the tone in the room, and fosters the collaborative spirit. If you're open, it's likely others will be too. If you exhibit a sense of play, others will play along. If you're tense and tight, so goes the day. The director needs to take responsibility for the atmosphere and the ambiance of rehearsal. If you are enthusiastic about the rehearsal, if you are energized and engaged, others will follow suit. If you are open to exploration and experimentation, of taking chances and risks, the actors will be too. If you are defensive and closed off, look out for the consequences of that behavior. The novelist John Irving, in talking about writing, said it was best to "be obsessed and stay obsessed." Your obsession for the play and the project will be infectious and carry over to the entire creative team—actors, designers and crew. Your care and concern for quality will be equaled by others on the team.

After each rehearsal it is a good idea for a director to sit down and think about how that rehearsal went. Review it in your mind. Replay the rehearsal. Contemplate it. Examine it. I highly recommended that the director *continuously* reread the play throughout the entire rehearsal process. Every day if that is possible. Most questions you have will be answered by rereading the play. Rereading the play takes you deeper and deeper into the source material and that is always a good thing.

A Note on Notes

Directors live by notes. In the research phase we are constantly making notes about the play, subjects to research, other plays by the playwright to read, random notes about the design, the characters, the staging and much more. Memory is fallible. We forget. So, writing things down is essential. It's like with dreams; if we want to remember our dreams, we better start keeping a dream journal.

The prompt book is the perfect receptacle for all of your notes, the place to keep your thoughts and action items organized and in their most powerful place—directly aligned with whatever is being referenced in the play script—and in your prompt book. You can also place your thoughts and impressions about rehearsals and the play behind the Journal tab in your prompt book. Your Journal notes become your daily diary of your directing experience with the play. This can be your private place to process your personal and creative journey on this production. It's a place where you can vent or you can gloat—and sometimes do both at the same time.

During the rehearsal phase we have the official rehearsal notes that are distributed to the production team. This happens daily. Oftentimes we may have a specific note that comes to us before a rehearsal or long after one has concluded. Sometimes it's in the middle of the night. We need a place for those notes, these action items. I recommend placing at the very front of your prompt book a set of the following form:

PRODUCTION NOTES

Production: _____ Date: _____

Director: _____ Page _____ of _____

SCENERY	PROPERTIES	COSTUMES

LIGHTS	SOUND	ACTORS/SM

You can adjust or make changes as you see fit. Each production may have a need for a special category of notetaking. For example, you may have an extensive use of projections in your production and would need a category to organize your notes for the projection designer. Or you may want a category for stage combat or choreography.

These notes are especially helpful when you walk into the costume shop or the scene shop to talk with one of the show's designers; you have your notes from the last several rehearsals right there in your prompt book. They become your directorial checklist. You can look over your notes and see if you need to talk to the costume designer about the color of that scarf that one character wears, or you can be reminded to speak with the prop master about the size of that vase that gets thrown against the wall in Act One. While you're at it, you might need a note to remind yourself to talk with the scene designer about the viability of throwing that vase against one of their walls.

Always walk into the shops with your prompt book! You never know when you may have to point out that on page 23 of the script the playwright actually calls for a red scarf for the protagonist as she throws a vase against the wall.

Here is an example of a notation system that can be used in the prompt book, especially for the recording of blocking, but also for notetaking during rehearsals, including technical and dress rehearsals. Feel free to create your own system. The important thing is to personalize your prompt book and to make it your own. Create your own shorthand, your own language, your own secret code that you can read and can use to communicate, on the fly, quickly and efficiently, the ideas that have come to you as you've prepared for rehearsal—as well as the ones that come during rehearsal.

When making notes in your prompt book, use a notation system, a form of shorthand. The goal is to write as little as possible but to record with as much accuracy as possible. There is rarely much free space in a playscript for all of your notes, but that is why directors have prompt books and why we have developed a left and a right-hand page system to hold all of your ideas about the play.

Use abbreviations to save on space. You can create your own symbols or use such traditional symbols as shown here:

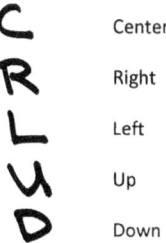

C — Center
R — Right
L — Left
U — Up
D — Down

Figure 9.1 Notation symbols.

Figure 9.1
(Continued)

S	Stage, as in DS for Down Stage
X	Cross
XX	Counter Cross
EN	Enter
EX	Exit
→	Arrows are used to indicate direction of movement
◯	Circles with "noses" indicate body position
FF	Full Front Body Position
¼R	¼ Right or ¼ Left Body Position
PL	Profile Right or Profile Left Body Position
¾L	¾ Right or ¾ Left Body Position
FB	Full Back Body Position
S↓	Sit
ST	Stand
⌒	When used between sentences or words, it means connect them
/	A slash between words or sentences means "a brief pause"
//	A double slash between words or sentences means "a long pause"
•3	Numbers indicate exact length of a pause in seconds, often used for cues
!	A new idea
__	A line under a word or line means to emphasize or stress
‾‾	A line over a word means to deemphasize or throw away
⌣⌣⌣	Laughing
f	Loud (forte)
ff	Very Loud (fortissimo)
p	Softly (piano)
pp	Very Softly (pianissimo)
————	Line across the pages indicates the beginning and end of a director' unit.
— — —	Dashed line across the page indicates a minor shift within a director's unit

Figure 9.1
(Continued)

Useful abbreviations for furniture include:

ch — Chair
fp — Fireplace
tb — Table
wd — Window
sf — Sofa

Special Fight notation can also be used:

+ Push
⊣ Pull
) Duck
(Jump
O Swing

For taking notes during rehearsal, including technical and dress rehearsal, the following may be used:

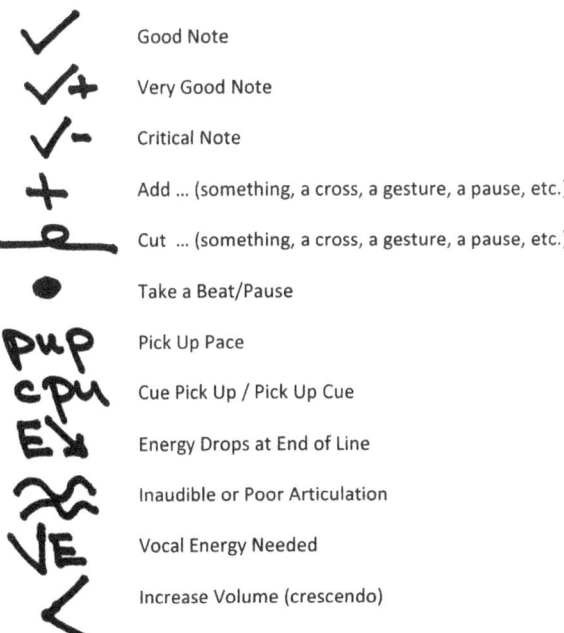

✓ Good Note
✓+ Very Good Note
✓- Critical Note
+ Add ... (something, a cross, a gesture, a pause, etc.)
⌐ Cut ... (something, a cross, a gesture, a pause, etc.)
● Take a Beat/Pause
pup Pick Up Pace
cpu Cue Pick Up / Pick Up Cue
E↘ Energy Drops at End of Line
∼∼ Inaudible or Poor Articulation
VE Vocal Energy Needed
< Increase Volume (crescendo)

Figure 9.1
(Continued)

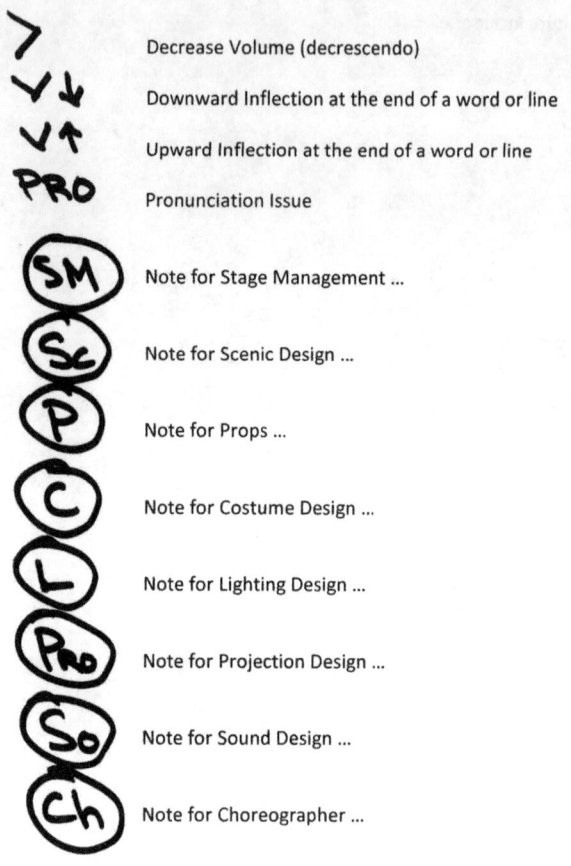

Decrease Volume (decrescendo)

Downward Inflection at the end of a word or line

Upward Inflection at the end of a word or line

Pronunciation Issue

Note for Stage Management …

Note for Scenic Design …

Note for Props …

Note for Costume Design …

Note for Lighting Design …

Note for Projection Design …

Note for Sound Design …

Note for Choreographer …

Here is a sample rehearsal schedule for Stephen Adly Guirgis's *Our Lady of 121st Street*. The key information being communicated is who is working when and on what parts of the play.

SAMPLE REHEARSAL SCHEDULE

OUR LADY OF 121ST STREET

REHEARSAL SCHEDULE

Week 1: Monday, September 08–Saturday, September 13

DATE	TIME	WORK	CALL
Monday September 08	5:30–6:00	Design Presentation	ALL ACTORS
	6:00–8:00	Read Through Table Work	
Tuesday September 09	3:00–4:00	Table Work	ALL ACTORS
	4:00–5:00	Block A1, Sc 1	B, V
	5:00–6:00	Block A1, Sc 2	Fr. L, RT

DATE	TIME	WORK	CALL
Wednesday September 10	4:00–5:30	Review A1; Sc 1 & 2	B, V, Fr. L, RT
	5:30–7:00	Block A1; Sc 3	F, G, I
	7:00–8:00	Block A1; Sc 4	B, N
Thursday September 11	2:45–3:45	Review A1; Sc 3 & 4	F, G, I, B, N
	3:45–5:45	Block A1; Sc 5	E, P, M
	5:45–6:45	Block A1; Sc 6	I, N, S
Friday September 12	10:00–11:00	Review A1; Sc 5 & 6	E, P, M, I, N, S
	11:00–12:45	Block A1; Sc 7	Fr. L, RT (B & P @ 12:00)
	1:00–4:00	Work A1	ALL ACTORS
Saturday September 13	10:00–11:00	A1, Sc 6	I, N, S
	11:00–12:00	A1, Sc 5	F, G, I
	1:00–2:00	A1, Sc 3	E, P, M
	2:00–3:00	A1, S1	B, V
	4:00–5:00	Run/Work A1	ALL ACTORS

OUR LADY OF 121ST STREET

REHEARSAL SCHEDULE

Week 2: Monday, September 15–Saturday, September 20

DATE	TIME	WORK	CALL
Monday September 15	4:00–6:00	Block A2, Sc 1	R, B, F, Fr. L
	6:00–8:00	Block A2, Sc 2	E, M, P (ADD G, F @ 7:00)
Tuesday September 16	3:00–4:00	Review A2, Sc 1	R, B, F, Fr. L
	4:00–5:00	Review A2, Sc 2	E, M, P, G, F
	5:00–7:00	Block A2, Sc 3	R, I, V, E, S, G, B
Wednesday September 17	4:00–5:00	Work A2, Sc 1	R, B, F, Fr. L
	5:00–7:00	Review A2, Sc 3	R, I, V, E, S, G, B
Thursday September 18	2:45–4:00	Work A2, Sc 2	E, M, P, G, F
	4:00–6:30	Work A2, Sc 3	R, I, V, E, S, G, B
Friday September 19	10:00–12:00	Run A2	ALL ACTORS
	1:00–4:00	WORK TBA	ALL ACTORS
Saturday September 20	10:00–1:00	Work/Run A1	ALL ACTORS
	2:00–4:00	Work/Run A2	ALL ACTORS

OUR LADY OF 121ST STREET

REHEARSAL SCHEDULE

Week 3: Monday, September 22–Saturday, September 27

DATE	TIME	WORK	CALL
Monday September 22	4:00–6:00 6:00–7:00	DESIGNER RUN NOTES	ALL ACTORS
Tuesday September 23 CAMINO LOAD IN LIGHTS	3:00–4:00 4:00–5:00 5:00–6:00 6:00–7:00	WORK A1, Sc 1 WORK A1, Sc 4 WORK A1, Sc 3 WORK A1, Sc 5	B & V B & N G, F, I E, M, P
Wednesday September 24 CAMINO LOAD IN SET	4:00–5:00 5:00–6:00 6:00–7:00	WORK A1, Sc 6 WORK A2, Sc 2 WORK A2, Sc 3	I, N, S E, M, P, G, F R, I, V, E, S, G, B
Thursday September 25 CAMINO	2:45–4:00 4:00–6:30	WORK/RUN ACT 1 WORK/RUN ACT 2	ALL ACTORS ALL ACTORS
Friday September 26	10:00–1:00 2:00–4:00	RUN ACTS 1 & 2 WORK TBA	ALL ACTORS ALL ACTORS
Saturday September 27	10:00–12:00 1:00–4:00	OFF	OFF

OUR LADY OF 121ST STREET

REHEARSAL SCHEDULE

Week 4: Monday, September 29–Saturday, October 4

DATE	TIME	WORK	CALL
Monday September 29	4:00–6:00 6:00–8:00	Run Through Work Act 1 as Needed	ALL ACTORS
Tuesday September 30	3:00–5:00 5:00–7:00	Run Through Work Act 2 as Needed	ALL ACTORS
Wednesday October 1	4:00–8:00	Run Through	
Thursday October 2 PAPER TECH 2:00 LIGHT OVER 4:00	3:30–5:30 6:30–8:30	Run Through Run Through	ALL ACTORS

DATE	TIME	WORK	CALL
Friday October 3	10:00 AM– 10:00 PM	121 TECH	ALL ACTORS
Saturday October 4	10:00 AM– 10:00 PM	121 DRESS	ALL ACTORS

OUR LADY OF 121ST STREET

REHEARSAL SCHEDULE

Week 5: Monday, October 6–Saturday, October 11

DATE	TIME	WORK	CALL
Monday October 6	7:00–11:00 PM	121 DRESS 2	ALL ACTORS
Tuesday October 7	7:00–11:00 PM	121 DRESS PREVIEW	ALL ACTORS
Wednesday October 8	6:30 CALL 8:00 GO	OPEN SHOW	ALL ACTORS
Thursday October 9	6:30 CALL 8:00 GO	PERFORMANCE	ALL ACTORS
Friday October 10	6:30 CALL 8:00 GO	PERFORMANCE	ALL ACTORS
Saturday October 11	12:30 CALL 2:00 GO 6:30 CALL 8:00 GO	PERFORMANCE PERFORMANCE	ALL ACTORS

OUR LADY OF 121ST STREET

REHEARSAL SCHEDULE

Week 6: Monday, October 20–Saturday, October 25

DATE	TIME	WORK	CALL
Monday October 20 LIGHTS LOAD IN	4:00	Pick Up	ALL ACTORS
Tuesday October 21 SCENERY LOAD IN	6:00 GO	1st DRESS	ALL ACTORS

DATE	TIME	WORK	CALL
Wednesday October 22 PAINT FLOOR	6:00 GO	2nd DRESS	ALL ACTORS
Thursday October 23	6:30 CALL 8:00 GO	PERFORMANCE	ALL ACTORS
Friday October 24	6:30 CALL 8:00 GO	PERFORMANCE	ALL ACTORS
Saturday October 25	6:30 CALL 8:00 GO	PERFORMANCE	ALL ACTORS

OUR LADY OF 121ST STREET

REHEARSAL SCHEDULE

Week 7: Monday, October 27–November 1

DATE	TIME	WORK	CALL
Monday October 27	OFF		
Tuesday October 28	OFF		
Wednesday October 29	12:00 PM	PERFORMANCE	ALL ACTORS
Thursday October 30	12:30 CALL 2:00 GO	PERFORMANCE	ALL ACTORS
Friday October 31	6:30 CALL 8:00 GO	PERFORMANCE	ALL ACTORS
Saturday November 1	6:30 CALL 8:00 GO	PERFORMANCE	ALL ACTORS

SAMPLE REHEARSAL GUIDELINES

OUR LADY OF 121ST STREET

Rules for the Road

A structure for the work

1. Don't be on time. Be early. Arrive prior to the stated call. Rehearsals will begin promptly. Be ready to work. As Woody Allen has said, "80% of success is showing up."
2. If you are going to be late for any reason, you must contact Stage Management or the Director.
3. Always bring your script and personal journal.

4. Bring a *pencil* to rehearsal. Keep it sharp.
5. NOTHING is permitted to distract from rehearsing the play.
6. Performers should not use rehearsals for memorization. Lines are due on September 15.
7. Stretch your muscles and warm-up ***prior*** to the call time.
8. Rehearse. Do not perform.
9. Bring water.
10. These are CLOSED rehearsals. Absolutely no visitors are permitted without the director's prior permission.
11. While the cast is working, there must be no noise in the rehearsal room.
12. Important: Keep your personal belongings off of and away from the stage floor. We need to preserve the stage space for rehearsal and for the free movement of the actors.
13. If you must leave the rehearsal room you MUST inform the stage manager or the director.
14. Stay focused on the work.
15. LISTEN! With your whole body.
16. Stay healthy. Eat well. Sleep. Drink water. Cut back/stop smoking. Cut back/stop drinking. Eliminate any drug use.
17. Do the *work*. Including the training work: Whatever we determine we need to do.
18. *Always w*ear appropriate clothes. Bring in—and wear—performance related clothing and foot wear as directed from Day One.
19. Work on flow.
20. Silence and Concentration are essential during the rehearsals. Be attentive. If you're in the room watch and support the work of all.
21. Communicate what needs to be communicated.
22. Respect the creative contributions of *every*one.
23. Be nice. But don't be afraid to defend your own creative ideas and sense of the work.
24. Don't put too much judgment on the work. Stay open.
25. Stay flexible. Things WILL CHANGE. Use an eraser.
26. "Be not afraid!"
27. "Keep breathing." "And moving." Keep the work physical. Find the play in the body. And Voice.
28. Remember: "Leap and the net will appear."
29. Stay awake. Stay aware. RESPOND.
30. Take care of each other.
31. Get obsessed. And stay obsessed.
32. No cell phones!
33. "Act Better!"

CHAPTER 10

The Director and the Stage Manager

One of the most important members of the Director's team is the Stage Manager, and a significant predictor of a successful production is often the quality of the relationship between the Director and the Stage Manager.

There are also two principal prompt books for any play production—the Director's prompt book and the Stage Manager's prompt book. Although they are very different in nature, purpose and function, these two books must talk to each other, communicate and interact with each other. Thus far we have been focusing on the Director's prompt book, but we also need to consider the function and interrelationship between the play's Director and the play's Stage Manager and how their two prompt books support each other and support production.

Here is a set of notes, mostly in outline form, on the role and duties of a stage manager, and on how a director can create a strong relationship with stage management and make sure that the stage manager's prompt book is in sync with the director's book. Any theatre organization's protocols or procedures presented to you as a director will supersede these notes, but these reflections and suggested protocols can provide valuable reference and guidance.

You should bear in mind, however, that the exact nature of the stage management position will vary from one production to another, and that there may be changes in the overall pattern of duties depending on each individual theatre operation and the nature of the play on which you are working. Some of these differences are mentioned in this document, others will become evident in the "working up" period of the production. When in doubt, encourage your Stage Manager to always discuss any issues or concerns with you. Develop a good and clear channel of communication with your Stage Manager and maintain it throughout the production process.

One of the dominant ideals of modern theatre is the achievement of a unity of all production elements, a harmony of acting and technical effects

- Stage Manager
- Assistant Stage Manager(s)
- Sound Assistant
- Music Director (if required)
- Choreographer (if required)
- Each Actor

In the academic environment, if the Director has placed scripts for pre-audition reading on reserve in the theatre's production office, remove these scripts for use in the auditions.

If the Director has made any revisions in the script, in accordance with copyright law, edit all the scripts accordingly. In the case of major revisions or cuts, the Director may be willing to have the cast correct their own scripts at the first rehearsal.

AUDITIONS

- Be familiar with the script, including the selections chosen by the Director for use in the auditions.
- Provide work-lights, necessary hand and set props, and piano (if required).
- Provide scripts and scores for the persons auditioning. Schedule the specific audition times for each actor.
- At auditions, inform actors when they are free to leave and if the Director wishes them to come to a later reading. Thank each person for attending the auditions.
- Announce when and where the call-back or cast list will be posted.
- Maintain quiet and order during the readings.
- Collect the scripts after the auditions.
- Secure audition area after auditions are completed (turn off lights, close doors, etc.).
- Be sure that a copy of the final cast list is distributed to each design department and every person on the production's contact list.

REHEARSAL SCHEDULE

- Arrange a rehearsal schedule with the Director.
- Check with whomever is in charge of scheduling rehearsal space, after having determined the Director's preferences, and also about any rehearsal report forms which are your responsibility to complete daily.
- Note other rehearsals or performances occurring in the building at the same time.

- Insofar as possible, following the Director's leadership, call the actors only as they are needed.
- Publish the rehearsal schedule for each week and post on the call board and/or any electronic distribution platforms used.
- Have each actor record the phone numbers and email addresses of the Stage Managers in their scripts. Announce that if an actor is ill or unavoidably detained, the actor should call the Stage Manager or Assistant Stage Manager immediately.
- If the rehearsal schedule changes, personally inform all actors, company members and department heads. Repost and republish the revised schedule.
- If there are major changes in the rehearsal schedule, especially if a run-through is cancelled, personally inform the Technical Director and the designers, and make the correct entries on the rehearsal report forms.

CONTACT LIST

Compile a contact list (with phone numbers and email addresses) of all actors and crew members working on the production.

The following persons should have a copy of the contact list:

- Director
- Producer
- Prop Master
- Marketing Director
- Box Office Manager
- Technical Director
- All Designers
- Stage Manager
- Assistant Stage Manager
- Assistant Director
- Musical Director
- Choreographer
- Actors
- Crew Heads
- House Manager
- Producers or Producing and Artistic Directors

Attend all production conferences with the Director in order to be familiar with the production scheme.

STAGE MANAGER'S PROMPT SCRIPT

As soon as the Stage Manager reviews his script, they should prepare the stage manager's prompt script.

- Copy the script in accordance with copyright permissions. Consider increasing the font size.
- Put the script in a loose-leaf notebook with blank sheets for notes at the end of the script. Use index tabs to mark each act and scene division, and to mark the location of contact lists, plots, etc.
- Mark the actor's entrances in blue pencil, and also mark warnings for these entrances about two pages before the actual entrance.

The prompt script should contain:

- Email and telephone list
- Rehearsal and Production Meeting Reports
- Rehearsal Schedules
- Attendance Chart
- Entrance-Exit Chart
- Preliminary Costume Chart
- Preliminary Property List
- Preliminary Light Plot
- Preliminary Sound Chart
- Ground Plans for each setting
- Notes on any sessions where the Director gives commentary, for instance, on characterization, regional accents, etc.
- A Supply of Blank Paper for making notes

TECHNICAL PLOTS

The following technical plots and charts discussed here are examples; it is the responsibility of the Stage Manager to confer early with the Director and the Technical Director to determine the necessity of each or all of these technical plots and the appropriate sequence of their preparation.

Entrance-Exit Chart

This chart is a useful reference for the Stage Manager for determining when actors will be needed for rehearsals and for determining which scenes can be rehearsed with a certain combination of actors. For musicals, make a separate chart for all musical numbers to facilitate calls for singing and dancing rehearsals.

Property List

A descriptive property list is prepared by the Stage Manager containing all specifications of each property needed. If there is any dialogue referring to a property that may help to describe it, this should be included. For the purpose of this list, assume that the person in charge of properties has never read the script.

For example:

- Small metal box: about 3" square by 2" high. Must fit into Will's raincoat pocket (Act I, Scene 3). Has a latch with a lock. Should look expensive, silver or gold, etc.
- Contents of wooden box: pair of gold cufflinks, small USB thumb drive. Thumb drive must be colored "RED" (see page 21 of play).
- Vase: not too big, about 4" diameter, 6" high. Should not look like crystal, "That's not a crystal vase, it looks like plain glass."

Copies of this property list are given to the Scene Designer, Technical Director and Properties Head after it has been approved by the Director.

Preliminary Property Plot

This plot indicates the placement of all set props, hand props and costume props (unless worn) for each scene. Copies of this plot are furnished as above.

Preliminary Costume Plot

This plot indicates the main garments and accessories worn by the actors in each scene. Any specifications mentioned in the script are noted. A copy of this plot is furnished to the Costume Designer.

Preliminary Sound Plot

This chart includes all sound effects indicated by the script, and others which the Director may have requested. It also indicates incidental music other than that which will be live. Describe the effects as precisely as possible. A copy of this chart is furnished to the Technical Director and to the Sound Designer.

Preliminary Lighting Plot

If any lighting effects are indicated in the script, the Stage Manager should prepare a descriptive list of these effects. This list should include any necessary practical lighting fixtures and their location on stage. Copies of this plot are furnished to the Lighting Designer and the Technical Director after being approved by the Director.

Preliminary Master Cue Sheet

This plot lists all cues with which the Stage Manager is concerned. All direct cues that may closely affect indirect ones; such as a cue for lighting which is taken directly from the action by the light board operator, but which must be timed with a cue for sound. After technical rehearsal, the cues from this master cue sheet are entered into the prompt script at the appropriate places. Direct cues are those taken directly from the lines or actions on the stage. Indirect cues are those which are transmitted through some intermediary, usually the Stage Manager.

EARLY REHEARSAL PERIOD

Read Through and Table Rehearsals

The first rehearsals are usually read throughs or table rehearsals. Before the first rehearsal takes place, the Stage Manager should:

- Check to see that all actors have initialed the cast list, if a physical cast list is posted, indicating that they will attend the first rehearsal. If any actor has not done so, inform him of the time and place of the first rehearsal. With an online or electronic posting of the cast list, a different protocol will be followed.
- Reserve an appropriate space for the first read through.
- Inform all designers of the schedule of the first read through and invite them to attend.
- Provide enough tables and chairs for everyone at the reading.
- Inform all present at rehearsals that eating and drinking are not permitted in the theatre or any rehearsal room, unless part of the action of the play. The Stage Manager is responsible for enforcing the no eating/drinking regulations.
- Provide a whiteboard, computer or projector for the Director if they will be needed.
- Check attendance of actors. Inform the Director when everyone is present. If anyone is missing, try to locate that actor by phone. Actor lateness or absence should be noted on the Stage Manager's rehearsal report.
- Provide extra pencils and inform the actors that they are to bring pencils and paper to all rehearsals.

- Announce the rehearsal schedule for the next week.
- Arrange, with the approval of the Producer and/or Director any special rehearsals or meetings, e.g., Intimacy Rehearsals or Weapons Orientations.
- Ask each actor to report to the Costume Shop for measurements (at previously arranged times).
- Check with all actors to see that they do not have conflicts with regular rehearsals.
- Announce to the cast that each actor is responsible for making their entrances on time during rehearsals. The Stage Manager calls only the beginning of acts and scenes. If any actors have a legitimate reason for being in other parts of the theatre during rehearsals, however, the Stage Manager can have them paged individually. Actors must not leave the designated waiting area without informing stage management.
- Complete a daily rehearsal report for each rehearsal and have it submitted via email and/or posted electronically on the show's website by 8:00 AM the following morning.

Blocking Rehearsals

- Arrange a conference with the Set Designer. Obtain ground plans for each setting and find out how each unit of scenery is constructed so that you may prevent the Director and actors from planning any impractical business. Explain the operation of all practicals (doors, turntables, etc.) to the actors.
- Mark the ground plan to scale on the floor for blocking rehearsals. The marking must be done with authorized tape obtained from the Technical Director.
- Provide rehearsal furniture to approximate the intended set props. If anything other than the furniture stored on the stage for class use is needed, these items may be checked out of the property storage room from the properties assistant. The Stage Manager is responsible for overseeing the return of this furniture before technical rehearsals.
- Set up the rehearsal furniture in advance of the scheduled time for the rehearsal to start.
- Provide rehearsal properties as soon as the Director feels the cast is ready for them. The size and weight of the real property should be approximated. The Stage Manager can sign out rehearsal props from the Properties Assistant. As a general rule, do not expect to have the actual production props before pre-tech rehearsal. However, if there appears to be a handling problem with any prop, bring this to the attention of the

properties master and ask that this prop be available as soon as possible for familiarization.
- Check rehearsal costumes out from the Costume Shop. Normally, rehearsal costumes are used when they will affect the actor's movement or are frequently used in business. Clearly assign responsibility for all rehearsal costumes either to the actor concerned, or to a costume technician.
- If any actors will be wearing high-heeled shoes or any special shoes during the performance, ask the actor to bring shoes with the same height heels for rehearsals. If they don't have such shoes in their wardrobe, send them to the Costume Shop for help.
- Arrange for costume fittings, as requested by the Costume Designer.
- Check the attendance of all actors at each rehearsal.
- Take charge and begin all rehearsals on time. If the Director is late, and prior permission has been given, run through something that has been previously rehearsed. Correct the actors on all errors in business, movement and dialogue. Use the blocking recorded in the prompt script as a guide.
- If an actor misses an entrance, send someone to find the actor and read that character's lines, unless the Director wishes to wait for the missing actor.
- Be prepared to walk through the part of any actor not at a rehearsal.
- Correct the actors on all business, movement and dialogue, either during a scene or after it, as the Director requests.
- Prompt as necessary. Make notes of all errors in the text and call the actor's attention to these errors after rehearsal. Wait for the actor to call "line" before providing the correct line.
- Simulate all sound effects indicated in the script. Occasionally, a rehearsal recording will be provided by the sound assistant. When this happens, operate the sound box.
- Take notes on any technical specifications that the Director indicates, such as necessary pockets in costumes. Make a written memo of these specifications for the proper technical department. Keep a duplicate record of all such specifications. Also note any change in any of the specifications and notify the appropriate department.
- Enforce eating/drinking regulations.
- Keep actors quiet while they are off-stage.
- Encourage actors not to walk across the stage unnecessarily, and not to wait for entrances where they can be seen by the Director.
- Consult with the Director concerning visitors to the rehearsal, and handle appropriately.
- Store all rehearsal props in one of the prop cabinets after rehearsal. The Technical Director or appropriate staff member will provide a lock if one is not on the cabinet.

- Clear the stage of all rehearsal furniture. Store any furniture from the property room out of the way, tarp and leave a sign on it saying that it is not to be used for any other rehearsals. If part or all of the set is available for rehearsal and the Technical Director has given permission for it to be used, be sure that it is completely struck from the stage after rehearsal. Scene shifts may require the use of the actors. A scene shift crew will not be provided before first technical rehearsal.
- Before submitting your rehearsal report, make sure it is approved by the director.
- Make sure the rehearsal area is clear and swept, ready for rehearsals the next day or other uses of the space, such as classes in academic situations.

Program Copy

The Stage Manager collects the material for the program for the Theatre or Box Office Manager in charge of programs.

- Ask the Director for the program notes and the descriptions of time, place, etc., if being used.
- Ask the cast members to provide the correct spelling of their names as they are to appear in the program.
- Secure a list of all crews.
- Ask the Director, Technical Director and Designers for a list of any acknowledgments to be included in the program. Double check with those staff members in charge of lighting, sound, costuming, stage crew, make-up and properties for accuracy of designers' names, crew head and crew information (some last-minute alterations in crews may have been overlooked).

Immediately upon moving from auxiliary rehearsal rooms to the performance stage for technicals, take up all marking tape from the rehearsal room floor unless the space will be continued to be used for rehearsal.

LATER REHEARSAL PERIOD

Preparation for Pretechnical Rehearsal

In consultation with the appropriate staff personnel:
- Arrange a conference to discuss the sound for the production. The Director, Sound Designer and the Stage Manager should be present. This conference should decide which effects will be "live," which recorded, as well as intermission and bridge music. Arrange a recording session if

needed. After the recording session, the Stage Manager should time each sound cue, and add this information to the sound chart. Begin to record sound levels as soon as possible, or arrange a separate sound rehearsal.
- Check regularly with the Scene Designer to find out what props and set pieces have been added or altered as set dressing. Add these items to the property plot.
- Work out a shift plot with the Technical Director and the Scene Designer.
- With the Technical Director, verify the sequence of opening cues for each act.
- If act curtains are being used, ask the Director to indicate speeds and record this information in the prompt script.
- Record all indirect cues in the prompt script in lead pencil. After all cues are set (before final dress rehearsal), use colored pencil so that they may be easily distinguished. The following color code is recommended:

Blue	Lights
Black	Actors
Orange	Sound
Green	Curtain and scenery
Red	Stage Manager's Cues

- Have the Assistant Stage Manager make a complete duplicate copy of the Stage Manager's prompt book for themselves.
- Make a checklist of all vital matters that should be checked immediately before the curtain is raised on each scene. In productions not using a curtain, this list applies to items to be checked before the house is open to the public.
- Take necessary photographs of set configurations and property placements both onstage and backstage.
- Check with the Technical Director for information about any Stage Manager's communication systems. This information should be included on the checklist. Also check for proper switch positions relating to stage work lights, counterweight system positions, etc.
- Check to see that Crew Heads have posted crew call notices.
- Prepare a checklist for all actors and crew members to register their arrival at rehearsals and performances. This should be posted on the Call Board.
- Be present when the scenery is set up for the first technical rehearsal. Learn the procedure necessary for getting each unit into position. Check to see that all properties are ready.
- Prepare dressing room assignments in consultation with the Costume department.

- Post the assignments on the doors of the dressing rooms.
- Determine with the Costumer if any "quick-change" areas will be needed. Inform the Technical Director as soon as such determination is made. Such areas should be planned as early as possible in the rehearsal period.

FIRST TECHNICAL REHEARSAL

Prior to the first technical rehearsal you will need to schedule a paper tech. At the paper tech, the Lighting Designer, the Sound Designer, the Director and you will go through the script page by page, cue by cue. You will record the cues and warnings in your prompt book and will clarify the nature of all cuing.

First technical rehearsal is mainly a planning and organization rehearsal. Lighting, sound and scene-shift cues are set and rehearsed as necessary. Smoothness in handling the cues is normally left to second technical and dress rehearsals. Normally, this means the rehearsal will proceed "cue to cue."

- Check to see that crew heads have instructed their crew members of each individual's responsibilities.
- Check to see that the stage is ready for the opening of the play. Have all items that take up valuable wing space removed either to the scene shop or other suitable storage area.
- Instruct the stage and prop crew about warnings for scene shifts.
- See that the paging system is working properly and check by the sound crew.
- Set up the time with the light crew head for the light check. It will normally require at least 10–15 minutes to complete, frequently longer. During the light check, see that the stage is ready for the check (set in place, masking in place) and that all personnel except the light crew are kept off the stage. Sound crew should not conduct any equipment check-outs that might interfere with the light crew. This same procedure is to be followed for all rehearsals and performances.
- Inform the Technical Director when all crews are ready to begin rehearsal.
- Should the actors not be present for this rehearsal, be prepared to stand in for the actors for various cues as directed by the Technical Director or Lighting Designer. The Assistant Stage Manager may also be used for this task.
- During the rehearsal, give all indirect cues and crew warnings as noted in the prompt script.
- Keep personnel on stage under control and ready so that time will not be unnecessarily wasted.

SECOND TECHNICAL REHEARSAL

- Second technical rehearsal marks the beginning of the integration period for the actors and the technical elements of the production. Delays are common, and repeated rehearsing of particular cues is frequent. Tempers sometimes get short. It will be up to the Stage Manager to keep the rehearsal going forward and actors and technicians working in harmony.
- Before the rehearsal starts, introduce crew heads to the actors and indicate briefly their duties and where they will be stationed during rehearsals and performances. Stress at this time, the absolute necessity of punctuality on the part of all cast and crew members. If the actors have been presented and involved at the first technical rehearsal, this introduction should take place then.
- See that the stage is swept. Normal procedure is for the stage crew to sweep before rehearsal and performance, and the prop crew after.
- Instruct the actors not to leave the stage immediately after an exit. They should wait several minutes in the wings because a cue may have to be repeated.
- Instruct the actors as to where they should be when not required on stage. During technical rehearsals, the actors may be permitted to sit in the auditorium. Once dress rehearsals begin, actors should stay out of the auditorium and wait in the Green Room, back hall, dressing rooms or in the wings.
- Inform the Technical Director and the Director when the actors and crew are ready. If a dress parade or makeup check is part of the technical rehearsals, call the actors for this purpose. Normally, however, costumes and makeup will not be required before the first dress rehearsal.
- Check the volume of the paging system. Repeat all warnings twice.
- Stop the action on stage when requested by the Director, Lighting Designer, Sound Designer or Technical Director. Find a place in the script a few lines before the cue being repeated. When ready to proceed, ask the actors to begin at this point: "Actors, go." Record specific cueing direction in the prompt script.
- Keep cast and crew quiet backstage.
- Supervise scene shifts, checking the items on the checklist before starting the next scene or act.
- During the action, stay at the prompt desk with the headset on so as to be in constant contact with the auditorium. Send someone else to locate people.
- Attend any orientation or instructional meetings, if required, related to weapons (firearms, swords, knives, etc.).

DRESS REHEARSALS

- Dress rehearsals are the polishing steps in the production's development. Usually, there will be two or more such rehearsals.
- Run the dress rehearsals exactly like performances. There may be stops for technical adjustments, but make every effort to establish the performance rhythm and pattern.
- Keep a daily time sheet of the running time of the production during dress rehearsals by act or scene as required. Time scene shifts and records.
- Discuss with House Manager the running of the show and provide accurate running times. The House Manager will operate the house on the final dress rehearsal as under regular performance conditions.
- If there will be late seating of audience members after curtain, coordinate the appropriate place in performance where this will be permissible with the House Manager.
- Check with Costume and Make-up Designers as to:
  - Costume and make-up check prior to the beginning of rehearsal.
  - Costume and make-up instructions to the cast.
- For musicals, arrange with the Conductor the entrance of the musicians into the pit, storage of cases and set-up of the pit area.
- Collect all notes from the Director for technical departments and read them before distributing them to the appropriate personnel. Make any changes necessary in the prompt script.
- Arrange to collect and safely store the actor's valuables.

PERFORMANCES

Performance is the acid test of all the work that has gone into production during the preceding weeks. The audience deserves the best that the cast and crew can give. Expect and inspire the highest professional attitude. It is the Stage Manager's job to see that this expectation is accomplished.

Before Performance

- Check the attendance chart on the call-board. Actors should be present at least a half an hour before curtain time. In many academic situations performance call time is much earlier, often one hour and a half before curtain. Crew call times may vary depending on responsibility and the needs of the production.

- Before the house opens, check to see that the forestage is clear and clean if a curtain is being used, or that the stage is set and swept if there is no front curtain. The stage may also need to be mopped.
- Assist the light crew as necessary with their light check.
- If weapons are used in the production, supervise the transfer from their secure location to the prop person in charge following the established protocols.
- At least thirty (30) minutes before the scheduled curtain time, after the lights and sound have been checked, inform the House Manager that the house may now open.

From this point until the House Manager gives permission to begin the performance, the House Manager is in charge of the theatre.

- Give the half an hour call.
- Check all properties. Any properties that must be preset on a stage set not using a front curtain must have been in place before the house opened.
- Check all scenery.
- Give the fifteen (15) minute call.
- Warn and call the actors to the Green Room if the Director wishes to speak to them.
- Give the five (5) minute call.
- Check with the House Manager to ascertain the exact starting time.
- Call "Places."
- Start the overture, if one is being used, when everyone is ready. If the overture is long, it may be started before place is called. Never start the overture without permission of the House Manager.
- Give "standby" to all crews.
- Start the performance according to the sequence of cues in the prompt script.

During the Acts

- Record all necessary data on the time sheet.
- Stay at the prompt desk in the Stage Management Booth. Get someone else to run errands or locate actors and crew if necessary.
- Give all indirect cues as noted in the prompt script.
- Keep cast and crew quiet backstage.
- Keep unauthorized people out of the backstage area, wings and booth.
- Warn actors of entrances and other cues.

Intermission

- Remind crew heads to leave one crew member on station during the intermission. This job should be traded off during the course of the intermission.
- Supervise the shift. The Stage Carpenter and the Properties Master are directly responsible for directing the shift.
- Call the actors for the next act.
- Check with the House Manager before beginning the next act.

During intermissions, control of the theatre reverts to the House Manager.

- Do not begin the act until all crew heads have reported ready to begin, and the actors are in place.

Curtain Calls

- See that the crew heads carry out their post-performance instructions.
- The Director will have set the curtain call during a technical or dress rehearsal. Follow the established format exactly. Take as many calls within these procedures as the applause warrants. Do not "milk" the applause.

After Performance

- See that crew heads carry out their post-performance instructions. If required, see that the set is struck in accordance with the instructions from the Technical Director.
- See that the stage is swept.
- If weapons are used in the production, supervise the transfer from to their secure location from the prop person in charge following the established protocols.
- Be the last person to leave the stage. It is the Stage Manager's responsibility to see that the stage is ready for the next activity, be it another rehearsal or class the following morning. Announce any afternoon rehearsal, pick-ups, etc. to the cast and crews before they depart, if possible. If not possible, alert them to watch the call board or check any online communications.

Production Photographs

Photographs are normally taken after a performance near the end of the run.

- Announce to cast and crew the date and time of the photo session well in advance of the date. This date should be cleared first with the Producer

or Theatre Manager to ensure there are not conflicts regarding use of the theatre.
- Obtain a list of the pictures planned from the Director and Designers and post on the call-board and/or online. Give a copy to all photographers that will be present in an official capacity and to the Costume Crew Head.
- Note on the picture schedule when each actor should make a costume change, and when the scenery is to be shifted. In a multi-set production, the scenes are set in reverse order of performance.
- Call the actors for each picture. Find a line of dialogue to start the action, a few lines preceding the line which the Director has indicated for the picture.
- Call and supervise the scene shifts as needed.
- Do not dismiss any actor without the permission of the Director or official photographers. They may wish to take close-ups after the other shots.
- Maintain quiet backstage and onstage during the photo session and in the auditorium as well.

STRIKE

Strike occurs immediately after the final performance or on the next scheduled shop call.

- Check dressing rooms for personal belongings.
- Collect scripts, if required.

POSTSTRIKE RESPONSIBILITIES

- If you are working in academic theatre the Stage Manager may need to be prepared to submit to the Technical Director a written evaluation of crew head performances.
- Submit the Production Prompt Book to the Technical Director no later than one week after strike. The contents of the book are:
    - Program
    - Prompt Script (legible, containing all the final blocking and Technical cues)
    - Contact List
    - Property List
    - Property Plot

- Costume Plot
- Lighting Plot (obtained from the Lighting Designer; fold and clip into notebook)
- Ground Plans
- Shift Plot
- Check Lists (with photographs if used)
- Entrance-Exit Chart
- Time Sheets
- Master Cue Sheet (direct and indirect)
- Return All Keys

CHAPTER **11**

Four One-Hundredths: A Model One Act

Four One-Hundredths by Richard Hellesen is a short one-act play that will serve as a model to illustrate the three-column prompt book technique.

As you read through the play you will see the system at work, page by page, in its entirety.

I've marked this script to show you how I use my own system, but ultimately you will learn to make a prompt book very much your own, creatively organized and extremely effective to use in rehearsal.

A prompt book is constructed; it is built. And its purpose is to help you fully realize your vision for the play. In this prompt book example, you'll see my musings, reflections, abbreviated notations, confusions and contemplations, lists of questions, insights, muddles and mistakes—and much more.

I've tried to give you a glimpse into the full process of creating a prompt book. Keep in mind that it is always an ever-evolving personal process, so the work I'm placing here, by its very nature, although following the structure I've outlined in the previous chapters, is still somewhat incomplete, a little idiosyncratic and even a bit messy. Your book will be those things too—highly personal and unique, perhaps even slightly eccentric and peculiar. That's the way prompt books are. A prompt book is rarely, if ever, a pristine product. It doesn't need to be perfect or flawless; it can be a bit cluttered and scruffy. It's not a machine-tooled thing; it's handmade. If there's a coffee cup stain on page 21, it's because the director was up until 2:00 AM trying to figure out the blocking for a scene. If one page has some crazy hieroglyphics, that may just be code that only the director can decipher. The director's prompt book is a bit like a personal diary, something intimate, almost a secret document. No one will "read" your prompt book but you, so it can be written in a language that only you can read. Ultimately, however, it is a language that you must translate to many others—usually verbally, but sometimes pulled from to create other written communications.

The prompt book is your crutch and your staff. You lean on it to provide you with the information that will allow you to communicate your vision to the actors, the designers and, ultimately, to the audience. The prompt book supports and sustains you; it protects you and it serves as an emblem of your special authority as the director of the play. Carry it with honor.

As you read *Four One-Hundredths,* go back and forth between the left page and the right page. Look for the connections between what the playwright has written and how those words have been translated into a directorial vision within the system of the three-column work. No two directors will ever have the same prompt book for the same play. Each director's book will be different and inimitable, a singular expression of that director's creative mind.

Please find the prompt book for *Four One-Hundredths* at the end of this chapter.

PLOT OUTLINE

Aristotle, in his *Poetics,* discussed six elements of the drama—Plot (Fable/Action), Character, Thought (Idea/Theme), Diction (Language), Music (Melody, Rhythm) and Spectacle. Sitting at the top of his hierarchy was plot. One of the first—and most valuable—steps to take as a director is to create a plot outline of the play. This literally becomes the story, the action, the narrative that the director *must* communicate. You can't tell a story if you don't know what that story is, and the best way for a director to know the story is to actually write out a plot outline of the play. It is the ultimate way to distill and deepen your understanding of the specifics of the play's storytelling.

It is important for the director to see the inherent structure, the division points, the hinges of plot, around which the story is constructed. The plot outline is based on the director's units that you have determined through your reading and analysis of the play. After the process of dividing the script into director's units is complete, the next step is to create a plot outline of the play based on these units.

To refine my understanding of the play's basic structure I've started by breaking this short play first into three parts—a beginning, middle and end. Then I proceeded to focus on each of the individual director's units. This is essential as it reveals the play's true narrative structure and distills and captures the very essence of the play's action, unit by unit. In order to do this, you simply write a one or two sentence description of each unit.

Each numbered plot description defines, in as simple and as straightforward a manner as possible, it's corresponding director's unit.

Here is my Plot Outline for our model one-act *Four One-Hundredths*.

FOUR ONE-HUNDREDTHS PLOT OUTLINE

THE BEGINNING (Act 1)
In a photographer's studio

1. Phil **shoots photos** of Sheila as Denny **philosophizes** about the "Human Drama of Athletic Competition.
2. Phil quickly **changes lenses** and **stalls** Sheila on her **request** for a break.
3. Phil **resumes shooting** as Denny **babbles** on in a humorous and self-promoting style.
4. Denny **makes a verbal pass** at Sheila as Phil **deflects** it in a light way, "Valvoline."
5. They **take a break** and Sheila **shares a brief personal exchange** with Phil about the shoot.
6. Denny **does a stroke job** on Sheila telling her how great she is and how much money they'll make together.
7. As Sheila **makes an off-hand remark** about the "heaviness" of winning the medal and then talks about her **plans and dreams for the future**, working with children who can't swim.
8. Denny takes Phil aside and **expresses his concern** that Sheila is too stiff; Phil **dismisses** him.
9. They **talk** about the **business** deal of who gets the prints and Denny **reveals** he's made a **trade** and has "speedos."

THE MIDDLE (Act 2)

10. The **shoot restarts** with Phil **encouraging** Sheila to be herself.
11. Denny **coaxes** Sheila into **revealing** what goes through her mind during a race and she **describes** a philosophy learned from her coach.
12. Then, at Phil's urging, she **recounts her race experience** at the Olympics. As she **opens up**, Phil **finds** the shots he's been looking for.
13. Then Sheila **mentions** she "almost" won the race.
14. Denny **sharply questions** her about "almost" catching the other swimmer in the race, and he **stops** the photo session. He grabs Sheila's medal and **demands** an **explanation**. She **tells** him it is a bronze medal.

15. Denny **explodes** angrily, **denouncing** her and **despairing** over his predicament. He **orders** her to stay and **exits** to make a phone call.

THE END (Act 3)

16. Phil **attempts to soften** the situation by **offering** to give Sheila copies of the prints.
17. They **talk** about the other swimmers who lost.
18. Sheila sharply **questions** Phil about his role as a person of the media and what he wants. Phil **responds,** telling her he wants to **capture** their souls in his images.
19. Sheila says he's out of luck—he's missed her soul—and she **exits**.
20. Denny meanwhile **rants** on the phone to Mark about his loss of money and the raw deal as Phil, **humming** the Star-Spangled Banner, **unlocks** his camera, **exposes** the film and **releases** Sheila's soul, her 3%—setting her free.

You can also use this Plot Outline to create a Fever Chart. A Fever Chart is a visual representation of the play's rising and falling action. It charts the ups and downs of dramatic action and helps us visualize, director's unit by director's unit, the path of the plot. From the early exposition to the point of attack scene to the first and subsequent complications to the crisis to the climax to the resolution, we journey through the action of the play.

It has been observed that each new high should be higher than the previous, and each new low no lower than the last, thus achieving the classic rising action of the play. In traditional dramatic structure, the highest point is the climax and the lowest point is the very beginning of the play, followed by the resolution.

For *Four One-Hundredths* it would look like this:

THE BEGINNING (Act 1)
In a photographer's studio

1. Phil **shoots photos** of Sheila as Denny **philosophizes** about the "Human Drama of Athletic Competition."
2. Phil quickly **changes lens** and **stalls** Sheila on her **request** for a break.
3. Phil **resumes shooting** as Denny **babble**s on in a humorous and self promoting style.
4. Denny **makes a verbal pass** at Sheila as Phil **deflects** it in a light way, "Castrol."
5. They **take a break** and Sheila **shares a brief personal exchange** with Phil about the shoot.
6. Denny **does a stroke job** on Sheila telling her how great she is and how much money they'll make together.
7. As Sheila **makes an off-hand remark** about the "heaviness" of winning the medal and then talks about her **plans for the future,** working with children who can't swim.
8. Denny takes Phil aside and **expresses his concern** that Sheila is too stiff; Phil **dismisses** him.
9. They **talk** about the **business** deal of who gets the prints and Denny **reveals** he's made a **trade** and has "speedos"

THE MIDDLE (Act 2)

10. The **shoot restarts** with Phil **encouraging** Sheila to be herself
11. Denny **coaxes** Sheila into **revealing** what goes through her mind during a race and she **describes** a philosophy learned from her coach
12. and then at Phil's urging she **recounts her race experience** when she was in the Olympics. As she **opens up**, Phil **finds** the shots he's been looking for.
13. Then Sheila **mentions** she "almost" " won the race.
14. Denny **sharply questions** her about "almost" catching the other swimmer in the race, and he **stops** the photo session. He grabs Sheila's medal and **demands** an **explanation**. She tells him it is a bronze medal and
15. Denny **explodes** angrily, **denouncing** her and **despairing** over his predicament. He **tells** her to stay and **exits** to make a phone call.

THE END (Act 3)

16. Phil **attempts to soften** the situation by **offering** to give Sheila copies of the prints.
17. They **talk** about the other swimmers who lost
18. and Sheila **questions** Phil about his role as a person of the media and what he wants. Phil **responds,** telling her he wants to capture their souls in his images.
19. Sheila says he's out of luck—he's missed her soul—and she **exits**.
20. Denny meanwhile **rants** on the phone to Mark about his loss of money and the raw deal as Phil, **humming** the Star Spangled Banner, **unlocks** his camera, **exposes** the film and **releases** Sheila's soul, her 3%--setting her free.

Figure 11.1 Fever Chart for *Four One-Hundredths*.

Some Additional Thoughts on the Play: The Dramaturgical Architecture of *Four One-Hundredths*

A play is a communication, and one of a director's first obligations is to make certain that the play communicates itself clearly and accurately to an audience. In order to do so the director must first analyze the primary source material—the playscript itself—and build their prompt book on that analysis. Only then can the fundamental directorial controls be confidently applied to achieve unity in the play's communication to the audience. Your prompt book has become the receptacle for these dramaturgical insights.

Richard Hellesen has given the director, in *Four One-Hundredths*, a structurally well-crafted play that readily lends itself to such analysis. And it is this analysis that goes hand-in-hand with the development of the Director's Prompt book.

Because plays reveal themselves primarily through plot, the director must first look to story to understand a play, and through a deconstruction of the elements of plot, come to a clearer understanding of the play's basic structure. Through a careful analysis of plot the director determines what scenes or moments should receive focus and emphasis.

A basic, one-sentence statement of the play's story can be extremely helpful to the director and can serve as a handle on the overall action line. As in diagramming a sentence, we are looking for the grammar of the play's action—a principle noun, verb and object. We are, in effect, attempting to uncover the basic ingredients of the play's plot. In this case, the noun is the play's primary character, the protagonist. The verb is the central action of the play, and the object is the play's main dramatic event.

Four One-Hundredths, for this director, is a play about a **woman** who **maintains her integrity** by **walking out** of a photo shoot. This sounds simple enough, but directors can—and should—further refine this one sentence description to enhance and extend their understanding of the play's communication. Add a few supplementary nouns, adverbs and adjectives and you can really heighten the specificity of the description. For example, *Four One-Hundredths* is a drama, with comic undertones, about a principled, young Olympic swimmer who preserves her personal integrity when she walks out of a tension-filled photo shoot after being confronted and berated by a slick promoter who discovers she won a bronze medal and not the gold medal he had thought.

There is it. In one sentence we have the story that must be told, and now the director must find the proper means to tell that story. Armed with this initial analytical information, the director moves on to answer other questions related to the play's dramaturgical architecture.

We start to look for and identify other parts of this dramatic puzzle. One such piece is the *inciting incident,* the pre-curtain event(s) that spark and fuel the action of the play. In *Hamlet,* for example, there are at least two such incidents: The murder of King Hamlet and the appearance of the Ghost, both events which have occurred before the curtain are raised and which are absolutely essential to the play's very existence. *Hamlet* could not exist without these two expository events. In *Four One-Hundredths* Sheila's Olympic race and Denny's negotiation with the off-stage Mark to promote and represent her give us our essential entry into the dramatic action of the play—and the major conflict between the protagonist and antagonist. Without either of these pre-curtain events clearly identified, the director cannot fully begin to approach this script because all action stems from and connects to these two events.

As the director reads and rereads the play, the various subdivisions of plot become apparent: Exposition, point of attack, complications, foreshadowing, crisis, climax and resolution. The identification of these plot elements is essential to the proper rendering of the play onstage, and they become the building blocks of your director's units as identified and created in your prompt book.

The director must also understand two other elements of the playwright's work: **the play's main dramatic question** as presented in the onstage action and **the protagonist's goal**, the major objective of the play's central character. All of the complications of the play—and the protagonist's goal itself—center on this basic dramatic question. In *Four-One Hundredths* this question could be stated as "Will Sheila preserve her personal integrity or will she be bought, packaged and sold by Denny"?

When this question is answered a play is over, and that answer is found in the play's climax. Classically, the climax pits the protagonist and the antagonist against each other in a final confrontation that resolves their basic conflict. At the climax of *Four One-Hundredths* the protagonist has a revelation about herself that resolves the play's dramatic conflict. The play's thought, the dramatic idea, is also most fully revealed in the play's climax. So, when Sheila picks up her athletic bag, and she exits, refusing to be bought, packaged and sold by Denny, we have the dramatic resolution of this story and our clearest insight into the play's meaning.

Because of its tightly crafted structure, Richard Hellesen's *Four One-Hundredths* gives the director a wonderful opportunity to experience the theatrical power of a finely turned and intelligently ordered sequence of dramatic action.

Properly defining the action, through the creation of the director's units as they are defined in your prompt book, provides the initial key to unlocking the play's theatrical structure and power. With a firm knowledge and understanding of plot, and the other dramaturgical elements of the play, the director can then provide, through the appropriate directorial controls, the proper emphasis that most fully communicates and realizes the play's dramatic values.

Translating and organizing this analysis inside your prompt book and then implementing it in rehearsal brings the play to life onstage.

Theme??

A blinding commercialism destroys humanity.

A blinding drive to commercialize destroys ones humanity.

To see only the dollar signs blinds us from seeing the person.

Subject: A person is more than is image.

Sacred vs. Profane

Real World vs. Ideal World

Body / Soul

Monetary Compensation vs. Spiritual Compensation

Exploitation

Finding True Values

INCITING INCIDENT(S)

(All Precurtain Events)

1. The Olympic Race

2. Denny acquiring Sheila in exchange for gymnist

THE PLAY'S MAIN QUESTION (PMQ):

Will Sheila's soul be packaged, bought and sold?

Will Sheila keep her soul, her 3%

Figure 11.2 *Four One-Hundredths* with three-column work.

Working out the Play's Main Statement: This is a <u>drama,</u> with comic undertones, about <u>a principled young Olympic Swimmer</u> who <u>protects her dignity</u> by <u>walking out of a photo shoot</u> after being confronted and berated by a slick promoter who discovered she had won a bronze medal and not the gold he had thought. Or maybe... <u>maintains her integrity</u>...by walking out.... Need to clarify this...

FOUR ONE-HUNDREDTHS

by

Richard Hellesen

QUESTIONS:

Can we strengthen S as the protagonist?

A stronger, more active goal for her, earlier?

A clearer Point of Attack!

Also...a more conflicted characterization—she has her own dramatic dilemma, she wants D to package her, sell her...?

Can her "conversion" take place more within the dramatic action through the staging?

LIST OF ADJECTIVES/
ADVERBS:

DENNY: Hyper, Crude, Greasy, Slick, Sadistic, Greedy, Wheeler-Dealer, "Agent", Street, Sleazy, Hustler, Sexist, Fast and Loose, Greedy, Unhealthy, Unprincipled, Vulgar, Dirty.

PHIL: Artistic, Friendly, Warm, Thoughtful, Kind, Caring, Nice Guy, Protective, Brotherly, Professional, Good, Ethical, Moral.

SHEILA: Innocent, Smart, Young, Clean, Shy, Stiff, Disciplined, Principled, Strong, Committed, Spiritual, Idealistic, Healthy, Process Oriented, Driven, Humble.

Possible Ways to Approach Character, Costume, Movement:
DENNY: OIL/DIRT; BEAST
PHIL: LIGHT/AIR; BIRD

SHEILA: WATER; FISH (out of water)

PLACE:

Modern, Hip, Angular, Metallic, Sterile, Cool, Antiseptic, Cold, Bright,

Possible Animal Observation Exercise Ideas

Beast/Bird/Fish

May also be reflected in Character Movement and Blocking Patterns

Hospital Room, Lab, Dissection, Processing Plant, Manufacturing Plant, Vacuum, Operating Room

Figure 11.2 (Continued)

CHARACTERS

DENNY, 28. Wears a light suit, tie askew; smokes fashionable cigarettes, has a fashionable haircut.

PHIL, 38. The garb of a working photographer; shaggy, prematurely grey.

SHEILA, 18. Short hair; wears a racing swimsuit with a large medal around her neck.

TIME

The present.

PLACE

A photographic studio.

Music? Playwright suggests Dire Straits, Twisting by the Pool??	**DIRECTOR UNIT #1** **TITLE: START OF PHOTO SHOOT / PLAYFUL PHILOSOPHIZING**	
Denny Smokes	PURPOSE: To Intro Characters, Set up Theme, foreshadow play's Climax / Denny's End point	BACKDROP FLASH UMBRELLAS PHOTOGRAPHIC EQUIPMENT LADDER BOTTLED WATER, SNACKS, ATHLETIC BAG WARM-UPS DIRECTOR'S CHAIR CAMERA
(Could start with lighting of D's cigarette—the "glow"		
ABC's Wide World of Sports Reference.		
Irony—inhuman packaging—antithesis of what is human	ACTOR OBJECTIVES	
Denny relishes the accident—the defeat—a submerged sadism at work.	(Can Shift and Change Within Each Unit)	
	DENNY: to recreate the details of the Wide World of Sports opening; to psych Phil up for the shoot; to make Phil Laugh	
Just like what will be happening to him—FORESHADOWING of end of play WHAM (see end of play)		LIGHTS DIM / SNAP UP
	PHIL: Get his shots	LIGHTS VERY, VERY BRIGHT. GLARE!
	SHEILA: Cooperate, give D and P what they want for the shoot	CLICK-WHIRR AUTOWINDS CIGARETTE
	ACTOR ADJECTIVES and ADVERBS:	
	DENNY: Hyper, Agitated,	
	SHIELA: Nervous	
	PHIL: Professional	
	INHERENT MOOD:	
	Energetic, Exciting, Caffeinated	P-CIRCLE D-STALK S-FROZEN / DEER IN HEADLIGHTS WHAM – SEXUAL GESTURE
Minor Complication—Sheila is tired and uneasy	**DIRECTOR UNIT #2** **TITLE: CHANGING LENS / SHORT BREAK**	

Figure 11.2 (Continued)

A MODEL ONE ACT

1

(A photographic studio, probably several floors up in a corporate office. Backdrop pulled down and spread out across the floor, flash umbrellas in position, other photographic equipment scattered about. A ladder or box on the backdrop, for SHEILA to pose on. A table at one side with bottled water, snacks, an athletic bag underneath, "USA" warm-ups thrown over a chair. At the other side, a director's chair in the shadows.

Music beforehand; actors move into place during end of it, setting up in character. SHEILA onto the backdrop, PHIL with camera ready to shoot, DENNY sitting in director's chair. Lights dim at the end of the music, then snap up. Bright light on SHEILA, arms in the air in a victory salute. The automatic "click-whirrr" of PHIL's camera throughout; PHIL ad-libs directions to SHEILA--"Beautiful", "head up", "out this way", and so on, occasionally stopping to fix her makeup, spritz her hair, pose her on the ladder, etc. Meanwhile, in the shadows, DENNY smokes and watches.)

S in place in front of backdrop

DENNY — DR

That's all I'm saying. Human. The Human Drama of Athletic Competition. OK? It's like, I don't know....The Guy. Remember? Every weekend, coming down that--what was it, ski jump thing? Hill? And you always see the end of it, when he goes crashing and it's just skis everywhere? But you know what you're thinking. "Man--how does that feel?" What's going through his mind?"

PHIL

(Stops, stares at DENNY)
"Whoooooooaahhh nooooooo..."
(Back to his camera)

D gestures   X US on angle w/P @ R

DENNY

Unh-unh--not at first. Not at the top of the thing. He's got to be thinking: a minute? minute and a half? to the bottom--score it just right, follow the groove, lean the right way, hit the take-off, nail the landing, that's it. And he gets the right start, he finds the right groove, it's all going perfectly--he's probably humming the national anthem, right? "Ohhh sayyyy caaan youuuu" WHAM. Up close and personal with some Norwegian fir tree. The Agony of Defeat Poster Boy.

DU #2

PHIL

Hang on. — X to table DL

	PURPOSE: To Show the beginnings of S's discomfort	
	S: to get Phil to stop shooting	
	P: to get S to hang in and give him one more shot	
	Adjectives/Adverbs:	
	S: weary	
	P: persistent	
	MOOD: Slight unease	
SALESMANSHIP: Irony –D can't sell defeat.	**DIRECTOR UNIT #3 TITLE: SELF-PROMOTING BABBLE**	
D is setting up his own dramatic trap because he is focused on the athletic, the physical (which he sees as the commercial) and not the human (the spiritual). This is his flaw.	PURPOSE: To focus on the irony of situation as played out later; to intro and extend thematics	
	ACTOR OBJECTIVES:	SNAP, SNAP OF CAMERA
Anthropology—only humans smile.	DENNY: To build himself up in P and S's eyes	
D can't relate to anyone—he is in the shadows. The shallowness of his values prohibits him from making human contact.	To "enlighten" them (world according to Denny)	
	SHEILA: To hide her discomfort from D & P	
Corn Flakes—Endorsement Contracts. Athletes on the boxes.	PHIL: To show S he is on her side	
"Buy" Me a Piece…. His true focus	ACTOR ADJECTIVES and ADVERBS:	
	D: cocky	
	S: uncomfortable	
	P: protective	
	MOOD: COOL and HIP and FLIP	

Figure 11.2 (Continued)

(Changes lenses)

SHEILA
(Starts to lower her arms)
Um....could I...

PHIL
Few more, then we'll break.

DU #3

DENNY
What I'm saying is, I could sell that guy, too. 'Cause it's not the Athletic part that counts. It's the Human part.

PHIL
OK, Sheila, big smile... —XR
(SHE raises her arms again-- snap, snap)

DENNY
It's the I Don't Know How It Feels To Screw Up That Bad, But I Know How It Feels To Screw Up, So I Can Relate thing.

PHIL
(To SHEILA)
Say "Corn Flakes"...

SHEILA
"Corn Flakes".

DENNY
(Which is just the flip side of the I'm Never Gonna Do That Great Thing, But I Know How It Feels To Want To Do It, So I'm Gonna Buy Me A Piece Of It thing.)

PHIL
Say "Wheaties". —XL

SHEILA
(Smiling in spite of herself)
"Wheaties".

FIRST COMPLICATION: D hits on Sheila Valvoline Inc. is an American manufacturer and distributor of Valvoline-brand automotive oil, additives, and lubricants	**DIRECTOR UNIT # 4** **TITLE: A (Not So Subtle) COME ON** PURPOSE: To show Sheila's initial bonding with Phil; To reinforce obnoxious character of Denny. ACTOR OBJECTIVES: D: To get "permission" from Sheila by flirting with her. S: To STOP Denny's advances ACTOR ADJECTIVES and ADVERBS: MOOD: Uneasy, Tense	
This is just practice? Not the real shoot? Would tensions/stakes be higher if this was for real? If the clock and the $s are running. Phil as "Coach" to Sheila = teacher, spiritual guide Phil=focus on feelings in contrast to Denny. Need sharp contrast in actors playing Denny and Phil in terms of type, temperament, tone.	**DIRECTOR UNIT # 5** **TITLE: : BRIEF BREAK** PURPOSE: Build the relationship between S & P ACTOR OBJECTIVES: P: to STOP Denny and RELIEVE Sheila by taking a break in the photo shoot S: to get into a conversation with Phil TO AVOID Denny ACTOR ADJECTIVES and ADVERBS: P: comforting S: relieved MOOD: Calm	FILM WATER. CIGARETTE TABLE
Sheila is outside of her realm—out of her depth, her	**DIRECTOR UNIT # 6** **TITLE: MOTOVATIONAL PITCH** PURPOSE: Increase Tension Via Physical Contact; Intro medal "issue."	

Figure 11.2 (Continued)

DU #4

                         DENNY —X DSR to stool

It's the I Wish I Could Get Inside That Swimsuit thing.
          (PHIL stops suddenly, stares at him)
Buuut...I'll Get As Close As I Can Get. Thing.

                           PHIL
          (To SHEILA, after a glance at DENNY)
Say "Valvoline".

                          SHEILA

"Valvoline"?

DU #5

                         PHIL XR to adjust umbrellas
Good job--take a couple while I change this.

          (Goes back to box, changes film) — as indicated

                         SHEILA
          (Relaxes for the first time)
I never knew how hard this was.
          (Stretches, shakes out her arms) — as indicated

                         PHIL
Wait 'til we get to the real shoot, you're gonna really feel it.

                       SHEILA
You sound like my coach... X to table, L

          (Goes to table, gets some water; DENNY crushes out cigarette and
          follows)

DU #6

                         DENNY
You're doin' great.

                         SHEILA
I hope so. I can't really tell.

4

102 A MODEL ONE ACT

"pool", seemingly not knowing good from bad	**ACTOR OBJECTIVES:** D: Build up S's confidence by flattering her; To get Shelia excited about possibility of making money. S: to make D see her as something more than just a product to be sold P: to kid S so he can MOOD: Cool, Rough, Tart.	WAGS MEDAL
Medal=Emotional Weight		
"Hurt me"—ironic foreshadowing of how she will eventually hurt him—in his pocket book.		
		TOUSELES HAIR TIGHT SMILE/TURN AROUND
D's focus—on "car"—the materialistic. **POINT OF ATTACK SCENE:** S, as protagonist, active toward her ultimate goal for the first time. True alignment against the antagonist (Denny). Leads directly to the play's climax and the answering of the Play's Main Question. (She announces herself, declares herself. Need to point this up in the staging and acting. More of a sense of squaring off against Denny.)	**DIRECTOR UNIT # 7** **TITLE: TALK OF FUTURE PLANS** PURPOSE: To show Sheila as a person of integrity and values—as human; to reveal conflict between D and S. ACTOR OBJECTIVES: D: To get S to open up in a personal way; Super Objective: to get her to sleep with him. S: to make D understand her goals/dreams	

Figure 11.2 (Continued)

Trust me. You'll sell yourself. The hills are alive with the sound of money.
           (Wags the medal a bit with his fingers)
That's really beautiful, by the way.

                        SHEILA

I know.

                        DENNY

Heavy sucker, too, idn't it.

                        SHEILA

More ways than one.

                        DENNY

Oh, "I'll bet".
           (To PHIL)
Every breakfast table in America. Hurt me like that, will ya? You.
           (Tousles her hair; SHE smiles at him tightly, then turns away)   **SX RC**

DU #7

So, what are you gonna do? Get yourself a nice car, maybe? Something like that?

                        SHEILA

I don't know. I haven't really thought about it.

                        DENNY

Well you better start thinking, 'cause you're gonna be swimming in it. Hey, Phil? "Swimming in it"?

                        SHEILA

I kind of want to use it toward college.

                        DENNY

But you're already--

                        SHEILA

No, I mean...after that. There's a, uh...couple of medical schools...

                        DENNY

Medical! Phil--
           (Points to SHEILA)

5

S: Helping others, her sense of gratitude, of giving back, of giving her joy in the water to those denied.

Research=Hard Work. Not the "easy money" approach of Denny.

ACTOR ADJECTIVES and ADVERBS:

S: sincere, personal

D: swaggeringly

MOOD: tense, sad

D: to flatter S; to get D's approval of his joke.

S: to set D Straight about her plans and who she is by being honest

D: to appear impressed so S will respond favorably

S: to make D/P understand her better by revealing her dream.

D: to make S think he cares so he can keep her in his stable and make money (false sincerity)

MOOD: Confrontational, Uneasy

UNWELCOME EMBRACE

WAGS MEDAL

Figure 11.2 (Continued)

                    (Nods, like "How about that?")
Like, what...sports--?

                        SHEILA
In a way....There's, um....this is gonna sound so weird...
          (An apologetic laugh)
There's lots of like kids, you know? Who can't....I mean, they can't even walk for--whatever reason....their legs...they can't just go swim? By themselves? And I just can't....
          (Shakes her head with a shy smile)
Anyway, there's all this research to do...

                        DENNY
Wow.

                        SHEILA
I just think every kid should be able to swim. By themselves.

                        DENNY
That is really...
          (Slight pause) —DXR to Phil
This is what I'm talking about, Phil. The Human Thing. I mean, a doctor, work with kids....We are gonna be so proud of you...

          (Arm around, a buddy hug--to SHEILA's discomfort)

                        SHEILA
We'll see.

                        DENNY
Nawwww--you earned it.
          (Wags medal again, then backs toward PHIL)
And you look great. Really.

                        SHEILA
          (Nothing else she can say)
Thanks. —XR to table for H2O

                        DENNY
Any time.

"Stiff". /. Not commercial SECOND COMPLICATION	**DIRECTOR UNIT # 8** **TITLE: DAMAGE CONTROL** *Directing the Director;* *Giving Direction* PURPOSE: Signal problems with Shelia ACTOR OBJECTIVES: D: to get P to coach S into a better performance P: to get D to back off by agreeing with him. ACTOR ADJECTIVES and ADVERBS: P: Mockingly D: Phony MOOD: "Stiff"	CIGARETTE
EXPOSITION: Denny traded a gymnast for Sheila the swimmer. "Bailed". A water term. To bail water—to keep a boat from sinking. For Denny this is a sinking ship. D sexualizes the gymnast— "arms, no butt". Always objectifying the women.	**DIRECTOR UNIT # 9** **TITLE: BUSINESS TALK** PURPOSE: to intro character of Mark and increase stakes for D. ACTOR OBJECTIVES: P: to get D to tell him what the "deal" is. D: to impress P with his negotiating prowess ACTOR ADJECTIVES and ADVERBS: P: inquisitive D: cocky MOOD: cool	LAUGH

Figure 11.2 (Continued)

DU # 8

DENNY
(To PHIL; quietly)
I think she's a little stiff.

X to Phil DR

PHIL
(Stares at him)
Stiff.

DENNY
A little. Any way you can get her to....loosen up?

PHIL
(Smiles ironically, and shakes his head; then)
"Sure Denny. I'll See What I Can Do."

DENNY
You're a champ. *XDR to jacket for cigarettes*

(Lights up another cigarette, as PHIL looks at him then turns back to his work.)

DU # 9

PHIL
Who gets the proofs--Mark?

@ chair DR

DENNY
(A disparaging laugh)
"Mark"....Mark bailed.

PHIL
Got this one to yourself, huh?

DENNY
First time for everything. Naw, we had "a talk". I tossed him the little--whatdya call her--arms, no butt? Gymnast.

PHIL
Goody for him.

DENNY
(Gazing at SHEILA)
New policy. Speedos are mine. Always.

7

This is the END of the BEGINNING and the BEGINNING of the MIDDLE. The equivalent of the end of "Act 1" of this one-act play and the beginning of "Act 2".	**DIRECTOR UNIT # 10 TITLE: COACHING THE TALENT** PURPOSE: To shift the focus, to prepare S to tell her story, her truth ACTOR OBJECTIVES: P: to get Sheila to relax by encouraging her to just be herself S: to sit down, eat lunch, LEAVE. ACTOR ADJECTIVES and ADVERBS: P: warm, personal S: tentative, unsure but positive MOOD: upbeat	
	DIRECTOR UNIT #11 TITLE: PERSONAL PROBING PURPOSE: to have S start to tell her story, humanize her. ACTOR OBJECTIVES: D: to get S to relax so she will photograph better ACTOR ADJECTIVES and ADVERBS: P: encouraging S: recollective MOOD: friendly, open, warm	CAMERA SOUNDS

Figure 11.2 *(Continued)*

Goody for you.

DU 10

(To SHEILA) — XC
You ready?

SHEILA

I guess.

DENNY

Let's do it! — sits in chair DR

(SHEILA takes her position; DENNY sits.)

PHIL

OK--like before, just relax, don't worry about poses, just be yourself...that's fine....

DU 11

(PHIL starts snapping away, but DENNY stops him with a gesture.)

DENNY
(Smiling, the genius at work)
So what goes through your mind?
    (Gestures to PHIL to resume shooting) — P roams D;L

SHEILA

Pardon?

DENNY

In the water, I mean. Before you start.   D moves S

SHEILA   DS

(As if he ought to know)
Mine starts on the blocks...

DENNY

Right, right, on the blocks. But it's still beat the clock, right? Two minutes--Go Go Go?

SHEILA

Actually...time just sort of...I don't know, stops.

D is focused on the competitive aspect—a race with a RESULT at the end—a winner and a loser S has a more Zen approach. Being There. In the Moment. Fully experiencing the Now. % "whatever" – the essence, the spirt, the....soul—and also the unknown		
	ACTOR ADJECTIVES and ADVERBS: P: encouraging S: recollective	
Phil sees her essence. He is the one, the catalyst that allows her to talk. He opens her up. S participated in a miracle—something that shouldn't have happed by all reason—but did. ENERGY=Must see a CHANGE in S. A GLOW D is getting mislead. The higher he gets, the harder he will fall.	**DIRECTOR UNIT # 12** **TITLE: RELIVING THE RACE** PURPOSE: To begin the process of revealing the truth of the bronze medal ACTOR OBJECTIVES: P: to get S to open up, to get her "whatever", her soul on film. ACTOR ADJECTIVES and ADVERBS: MOOD: recollective, comforting Physical memory=emotional memory	She SMILES. BEAMS Effervescence Glow Almost a Dance "Physically remembering it". Key to staging. The headshake of disbelief, but the reality is the accomplishment

Figure 11.2 (Continued)

                    (Slight pause)
It's a race.

                            SHEILA
I know, but...When you're in it, it's more like...you're there, but you're not there--you know?

                            DENNY
                    (He doesn't)
Unh-hunh.

                            SHEILA
It's like...OK, there's this thing my coach always says? We're seventy percent water. And the pool is one hundred percent water. So it's not like your body swimming--it's just this thirty percent of...whatever, that has to move through the water as fast as it can. So you're supposed to just...get the seventy percent out of the way. Let that thirty percent do what it can do. You don't really think about it.

                            PHIL
                    (Slight pause)
You remember it, though, don't you?

[handwritten: D rises X U;R]

                            SHEILA
Parts of it.

DU 12
                            PHIL
Tell me about it.

                            SHEILA
I don't know--it all seemed...real vague. Slow.
          (As SHEILA tells her story, PHIL begins to shoot--with occasional
          soft ad-libs, but ==he finally sees what he's been waiting for==)
It was such a....Maybe it was the challenge. I mean, I barely made it out of semi's--I wasn't even supposed to place. It was supposed to be this duel--the Hungarian girl, Haraszthy? And Jennifer Webber. Maybe Liang, but...that's Jenny's event, right down to her toes. I mean, she's built for it, she's trained years for it, everybody's telling her, This is it, you know? Records are gonna fall. And she's down there, and Haraszthy, and...and the crowd's all....Like, I can't even believe I'm here.

                            SHEILA (Cont'd)
          (Shakes her head--and begins ==physically remembering the race==)

[handwritten: — D Xs DR, sits]

9

"Almost caught her"—perhaps the most important line in the play. That which creates the crisis and leads to the climax.	S: to make them see her as she was at that moment; to share her experience with them. To have them know what happened to her in that pool.	
S: Did not Win Race 3rd COMPLICATION CRISIS POINT S: enhances the greatness of this victory for her—she "wasn't even supposed to place."	**DIRECTOR UNIT # 13** **TITLE: TRUTH REVEALED** D's Crash and Burn PURPOSE: Intro major plot complication/obstacle for D ACTOR OBJECTIVES: S: To Reveal the essence of the event to them P: to encourage her, to thank her, to make her give another "percent" ACTOR ADJECTIVES and ADVERBS: MOOD: Tense, Awkward, Dangerous	

Figure 11.2 (Continued)

drafting off of Haraszthy--but see, I was drafting off of Liang. ==Just letting it happen==. And I guess...Jenny just got a bad turn into the third leg, 'cause all of a sudden....I mean, half of me knew she was falling off, but the other half knew that I got a really good turn. The third 50 was....the best. The best. ==I could feel it, filling me up--this...energy==. Every stroke, every beat, the kick-turn into the fourth was right there, and I just....==there== I am, and there's the pad coming up on the wall, getting bigger and bigger, all I have to do is go for it...and I did it. I don't know how, but I did. Best race of my life.
        (Pause)
==And I almost caught Haraszthy. Almost caught her.==
        (Stands still, looking down at medal) — *S lowers arms*
Sometimes I wonder, you know, if--
        (Stops, then smiles)
But I can't really complain, can I?

                          PHIL
==Perfect.== — *P is close to S*

DU # 13

                         DENNY
        (Pause; quietly)
What do you mean, "almost". — *D rises*

                        SHEILA
        (Explaining it, as if he truly doesn't understand)
Well, I mean, they were right--the record did fall... — *D steps toward S*

                         DENNY
==No--what do you mean you "almost" caught her?==

                        SHEILA
        (A bit quieter, but still assertive)
See, I wasn't even supposed to place--

                        DENNY
No--I'm not talking about-- — *D steps toward S again*

                        PHIL
We're trying to work here, Denny...

10

	DIRECTOR UNIT # 14 **TITLE: A CONFRONTATION** PURPOSE: to square D and S off from one another; to portray P as protector/defender of S	D LIFTS MEDAL
	ACTOR OBJECTIVES: D: to force S into telling him the exact truth To get her to confirm the information P: to keep S from seeing or hearing his "snicker" S: to make D back off by defending herself	
Not Gold, not Silver—but THIRD PLACE – a Bronze medeal. MAJOR COMPLICATION ARTICULATED	ACTOR ADJECTIVES and ADVERBS: D: Angry, prosecutorial S: numb, faltering P: strong, protective, angry MOOD: hot, mean, rough, dangerous	D DROPS MEDAL P SNICKERS

Figure 11.2 (Continued)

DU # 14

                          DENNY
            (Moving into the light)
Phil? You mind? ——————   *D blocks P, XL*
                          DENNY (Cont'd)   *S D P*
            (Slight pause; goes to SHEILA and lifts medal)
What is this.
            (No reply)
What is this.

                          SHEILA
            (Simply)
Medal.

                          DENNY
WHAT IS THIS.

                          SHEILA
            (After a second, quietly)
Bronze. ——— *X away, toward table DL*

            (DENNY stares at her, then drops the medal and looks around,
             fuming, at PHIL.)

                          DENNY
You know that?

                          PHIL
            (Shakes his head, then)
Mark didn't--? — *XR, US of chair*

            (DENNY stares at PHIL, who just snickers slightly.)

                          SHEILA
I was close. — *turns back to D*

                          DENNY
How "close" were you.

                          SHEILA
            (Quietly)
Four one-hundredths.

"Use that"—utility, use

Function of Sales—to Sell

**DIRECTOR UNIT #15
TITLE: AN EXPLOSION OF ANGER**

PURPOSE: To show extent D's meltdown.

ACTOR OBJECTIVES:

D: to hurt S by lashing out at her, yelling at her

ACTOR ADJECTIVES and ADVERBS:

D: ballistic, irate

S: resigned.

MOOD: Violent, crude, hot, blaring

CAMERA SNAPS

Figure 11.2 *(Continued)*

I didn't ask what RACE you were in--

          SHEILA

Four one-hundredths of a second.

          DENNY

You lost by...

          PHIL

She didn't lose.

          DENNY

Pardon me. No. That's right. She did not LOSE. She got to stand on the LITTLE stand, with the flag that goes up SLOWER than everybody else's, and it's not her MUSIC, by four one-hundredths of a second--is that right?

          SHEILA
     (Faltering)
Yes.

          DENNY

Terrific. Just terrific.

          PHIL

Give her a break, man.

DU 15

          DENNY

A break. Give me a break. A BRONZE? WHAT THE HELL AM I SUPPOSED TO DO WITH THAT?! HUNH?! "FOUR ONE-HUNDREDTHS"?? HOW THE HELL AM I SUPPOSED TO USE THAT?! USE it? I don't even know what that IS! A blink of an eye? Half a blink? Half an eye?
   (PHIL points camera off in space and snaps) — *as indicated*
Oh, that much, huh?
   (Turns back to SHEILA)
WHAT THE HELL DID YOU DO?! One extra BREATH? One extra KICK? FILE YOUR DAMN NAIL THAT MORNING? WHAT THE FUCK YOU THINK WE'RE DOING HERE?!

          SHEILA
   (Barely audible)
It was the best that I--

		CELL PHONE
		JACKET
		DIRECTOR'S CHAIR
		DOOR SLAMS
This Unit is the structural END of the MIDDLE and the BEGINNING of the END, the equivalent of the beginning of the "Third Act" of this one-act play	**DIRECTOR UNIT # 16 TITLE: A SHOW OF SYMPATHY / EXIT & O.S> PHONE CALL**	CAMERA LENS
	PURPOSE: To show P on S's side.	SILENCE
	ACTOR OBJECTIVES:	D: YELLING O.S.
	P: to make S relax by injecting some small talk; to comfort S	MEDAL
	ACTOR ADJECTIVES and ADVERBS:	
	P: concerned, warm, caring	
	S: open, vulnerable.	
	MOOD: quiet, soft, gentle	
REVISITING THE PHYSICAL MEDAL		
		D: YELLING O.S.

Figure 11.2 (Continued)

IT'S NOT GOOD ENOUGH! **X to DR** *for jacket*
  (Stops, turns away, stares at ground, then)
OK, look--I gotta go make a phone call. Don't go anywhere.

  (Grabs cell phone out of his jacket pocket and exits, throwing over
  the director's chair and slamming out the door as he goes. — *as indic*

XT SR

DU 16

SHEILA —*@SL*
and PHIL look at each other; then PHIL goes to the side and begins
removing lens, etc. A long silence, then:)

PHIL
I, um...I can get you some prints of these, if you want. No charge. —*from* **SR**

  (DENNY heard yelling in the other room: "NO, goddammit, we're
  gonna talk NOW!" Slight pause. SHEILA looks at PHIL, then takes
  off medal.)

PHIL
What about...what's her name. **X to S SL**

SHEILA
Who.

PHIL
The Chinese girl.

SHEILA
Liang? Second.
  (Slight pause)
Fifteen one-thousandths.

PHIL
Jesus....She probably got shot for real, huh?

(DENNY off: "HEY! I gave you a fucking gold-medal gymnast!")

SHEILA
Quicker, anyway. **X to DR** *for her bag; sweats*

13

The "Agony of Defeat" as mentioned in D's first monologue Cruelty American Style	**DIRECTOR UNIT # 17** **TITLE: A DEEP QUESTIONING (GENERAL)** PURPOSE: To get Sheila to begin to strengthen and regain her sense of self ACTOR OBJECTIVES: S: To find out from P what/why she's been exploited P: to please her, to be gentle with her, by answering truthfully. ACTOR ADJECTIVES and ADVERBS: S: strong, knowing P: compassionately, gently MOOD: realistic, clear, truthful	SWEATS DENNY: O.S. VOICE
Hereoes Destoryed by Media Why "you" do it. Making it direct and personal. Get the shot, the story. D=scavenger—sex without love, money without work, feeds off others KEY LINE: PLOT POINT CLARIFIED IN DIALOGUE	**DIRECTOR UNIT # 18** **TITLE: A DEEPER QUESTIONING (PERSONAL)** PURPOSE: To express the direct and honest relationship between P & S; express the strength of S through her exit ACTOR OBJECTIVES: S: to see if P is one of "them" P: to make S see his humanity, to bond with her	DENNY: O.S. VOICE MAKE A MAJOR VISUAL MOMENT OF HER TAKING OFF THE MEDAL.

Figure 11.2 *(Continued)*

DU 17

                              SHEILA
        (Begins putting on sweats; a bit sharp)
So which is it? That I didn't win, or I didn't lose big enough?

                              PHIL
Either one. *—sits on stool @DL table*

                              SHEILA
Well. That explains it.

                              PHIL
What.

                              SHEILA
After the race? When we got out of the water? Where do you think the cameras were?
        (DENNY off: "Fuck you, Mark!")
Come on--you're a photographer. Where would you be? *X to Phil*

                              PHIL
        (Considers, then:)
Jenny Webber. *P seated on stool; S stands over him*

                              SHEILA
"Gosh Jenny, what happened? This was supposed to be your best race--how did you manage to end up sixth? Where do you think you screwed up?" Right in her cold wet face. They had her in tears.

DU 18
        (Pause)
Why do you do it?
        (DENNY off: "That's a lie and you know it!")
I mean, what do you people want?

                              PHIL
He wants something that-- *—X away*

                              SHEILA
I know what he wants. I'm talking about you. He's nothing without you, right? *—X D;R*

                              PHIL
He calls the shots.

14

	ACTOR ADJECTIVES and ADVERBS: P: honestly, directly S: strongly, boldly MOOD: somber, sharp, decisive	PAUSE
SHE EXITS: THE CLIMAX She refuses to be commodified, to be packaged and sold.	**DIRECTOR UNIT # 19 TITLE: HER TRIUMPHANT EXIT** PURPOSE: To Highlight the play's CLIMAX ACTOR OBJECTIVES: S: To make D recognize her strength of character. ACTOR ADJECTIVES and ADVERBS: S: boldly, proudly, strongly MOOD: heroic, bold, strong	D: O.S. YELLING

Figure 11.2 (Continued)

Come on, Phil--you're the one in the pool. What are you doing here?

PHIL
(Looks at her, considering, then:) —Rises from stool
There are these tribes--in some parts of the world...they won't let you photograph them. They believe that the camera takes a small piece of their soul, and burns it into the film.
(Slight pause)
I keep trying to prove that they're right. —X to S

SHEILA
You think that's in there? My soul?

PHIL
I don't know. Maybe a...glimpse of that thirty percent. If I'm lucky.

SHEILA
So you can sell it off, huh?

PHIL
(Pause)
Like he says.... It's the We All Need Something Bigger Than Life thing.

SHEILA
Whose life.

PHIL
Everybody's.

DU 19

SHEILA
Then I guess you're out of luck. 'Cause the only life I was "bigger than" for two minutes was mine--and that's back in the pool. Not around my neck. Sorry that's not enough.
(Drops medal in bag)
Keep the prints, Phil. There's nothing there. — DIAGONAL
(DENNY off: "What am I supposed to do, take that to a client?
BULLSHIT!" SHEILA picks up athletic bag, starts out, then turns)
Missed me by that much.

(SHE's gone. EXITS OFF DL

15

P did catch her soul. Then he let her go.	**DIRECTOR UNIT # 20 TITLE: DESTROYING THE FILM** PURPOSE: To show P's ultimate character. ACTOR OBJECTIVES: P: to tidy up, close down the shoot—and destroy the film; to thwart D, to side with S ACTOR ADJECTIVES and ADVERBS: P: professional, carefree, happy, satisfied D: vindictive, angry, sarcastic MOOD: Chaotic, frazzled, blaring, glaring. D: to force Mark to give back the gold medalist gymnast.	EQUIPMENT CAMERA FILM HUMMING THE NATIONAL ANTHEM CAMERA LENSES MAJOR ACTION: DESTROYING THE FILM
WHAM—recalls the skier from D's first monologue. P is like that ski jumper, on the edge of the abyss, poised for victory or defeat.		
P has destroyed the film, the preciousness that cannot be shared. Valuing the HUMAN above the COMMERCIAL D=left in the hell of his own making.	**DIRECTOR UNIT # 21 TITLE: WHAM! THE AGONY OF DEFEAT** PURPOSE: to show D's loss; to express S's absence ACTOR OBJECTIVES: D: to get P and S to help him salvage his situation by presenting a new plan P: to save himself, to participate in S's mystery, to put an end to his relationship with D, to turn out the lights—literally and figuratively. ACTOR ADJECTIVES and ADVERBS: P: methodical, self-satisfied, smug D: Pitiful, alone, lost MOOD: triumphant, joyous	PHONE DROP PHONE SOCKET FLASH UMBRELLAS CAMERA FLASH BLACKOUT

Figure 11.2 (Continued)

A MODEL ONE ACT   125

DU 20

A moment; PHIL looks after her as DENNY raves on,
          with varying audibility offstage.)

DENNY	PHIL
(Off)	
NO--Who's in the meeting saying, Oh, I think we should let Denny handle one by himself, I think it's time DENNY gets to take a shot--and what? All the time you're scamming everybody?	(HE begins tidying up his equipment. HE listens to DENNY for a moment, thinking. HE stops, looks at the camera, then off to where DENNY is. Pause; then HE pops the back of the camera open. Mildly:)
	"Whooooah noooooooo."
Look...look...don't you...You SAT there, you son of a bitch!...."Build a campaign around her"?! YOU CAN'T BUILD SHIT ON SOMETHING LIKE LIKE THIS, AND YOU KNOW IT!....	(HE pulls the film out, and begins humming the national anthem. HE packs up the camera, puts lenses away, whatever. Then, still humming the national anthem, he zips the film out like a streamer and tosses it on the floor.—as indic **/SL**

DU 21

DENNY storms in) — enters from **R**

DENNY
(Still on the phone)
...Beer?? A BEER COMMERCIAL? What do you think I got here, some volleyball player?!....Right--fine--you get ten bimbos for scale and you do that. WE TALKED WORLD-CLASS, AND I WANT WORLD-CLASS, goddammit!....
          (HE's on the drop, center, looking around for SHEILA but still raging
          into the phone; PHIL heads for the socket where the flash umbrellas
          are plugged in.)
Will you just...What are you trying...Look, WHERE THE HELL DOES THIS LEAVE ME?!

          (PHIL sets the flash off; DENNY is momentarily frozen in the light,
          mouth open, panic on his face.)   **LQ**

                              PHIL   **LQ**
"Wham."
          (HE pulls the plug. Blackout.)   **SQ**

                         END OF PLAY

CHAPTER 12

Final Thoughts

I hope you have discovered, through this system of developing a three-column prompt book, a useful tool to help you achieve your directorial visions for the plays you choose to direct. Creating a truly great prompt book can be a lot of work but also a labor of love—a gift to all of your collaborators and to your audiences.

As the Hollywood studio executive, Joe Roth, said "Everybody wants to go to heaven, but nobody wants to die to get there." We all want to get to opening night with a great show, but, sometimes, we don't realize just how much we have to give of ourselves to do that. How many times do we have to read the script to unlock its secrets? How many late-night hours do we need to spend pouring over our prompt book in preparation for that first rehearsal? At times, directing a play—and putting together your prompt book—may feel like a little death, but if you've done the work, and you will have done the work if you follow this system, nothing can be more rewarding. You too can go to Director Heaven!

Another Hollywood legend, actress and producer Sandra Bullock, offers this great advice: "If I'm going to be held responsible, I'm going to be responsible." Believe me, as the director of a play, you are going to be held responsible! You need to embrace that fact; you are the number one person responsible for the success or failure of a production. Your main responsibility then is to creatively shepherd the show from first rehearsal to opening night by directing well—and I firmly believe that putting together a strong and effective prompt book is your best assurance of having a successful directing experience. Creating a well-conceived, well-organized and theatrically potent prompt book is, in many ways, your first responsibility—and the one that will mightily contribute to your accomplishments as a director. Be responsible by creating the best prompt book you can.

My intention has been to provide an organizational and interpretive method that allows you to just that, to creatively coordinate and focus your intent—and achieve success in directing plays.

A well-developed prompt book can be your blueprint, your road map, and your guide. It can be the compass that lets you know when you may be veering off course or headed in exactly the right direction, and it can help you realize your goals for the play.

One of my mentors, the great American acting teacher and director Milton Katselas, said that the goal of the theatre artist was "to have the technical ability to create what is needed to express fully to an audience the highest possible communication, create the desired emotional response upon the audience and bring understanding to them." Your prompt book, in part, defines your technical ability and, combined with your skills and your talent, allows you to attain this highest level of communication and to achieve these great artistic goals as a stage director.

Make a friend of your prompt book. It can be your cheat sheet (it contains all of your ideas and insights into the play at the ready) and your guiding light. Respect the work you've done to create it. It is a repository, a true storehouse, of all your thoughts, understandings and dreams about the play. Keep it close at hand. Read through it often. It will keep you honest. It will remind you of your original sense of purpose for the play. It will make you a better collaborator as it helps you effectively and efficiently communicate its content to actors and designers. It will bring you closer to the playwright and help you become more intimate with—and truer to—the intent of the playwright's words. It is also your bridge to reach and deliver the full measure of the play's meaning and intent to the audience.

The prompt book also helps you gain access to the physical life of the play onstage. It's where you first make determinations and decisions about how an audience will experience the play—what an audience will *see* and what an audience will *hear*.

A strong prompt book allows the director to organize the play for rehearsal and make workable, practical and theatrical sense of the play. It allows the director to arrange and structure the rehearsal process in an effective, meaningful and creative way. It makes you better prepared to enter into—and complete—the process of production.

A well-constructed prompt book is the best assurance of a successful directorial outing. Perhaps its strongest feature is as the guiding force that unites the director and the play, the director and the playwright, the director and the actors, the director and all of the many artistic contributors of the production—and, ultimately, the director and the audience.

May the exciting and thrilling theatre in your head be transformed into a vibrant and rich theatre on the stage.

Index

Note: Page numbers with *italic* for figures and **bold** for tables.

adjectives/adverbs 20
after performance 82; *see also* performance
Allen, W. 64
antagonist 12, 91
anticipation 50–51, 53
appearance *see* order of appearance
Aristotle 8, 86
artistic success for prompt book *see* prompt book
assistant stage manager 53, 70, 77, 78; *see also* stage manager
auditions 69; materials 19; organization of 67; passages 19; scripts for 69; stage managers in 68

before performance 80–81; *see also* performance
blocking 44–48; notation 34, 36; paper 34, 46; preliminary 20; rehearsals 46, 74–76
BMW 22–23
boiling process 23
Bridges, M. 2
Bullock, S. 126
business 19

Caesar, J. 31
Carnegie Mellon University 3
Carra, L. 3–5, 50
cast of characters 7
character five 8
character objectives 20
chart 71–72, 88, *89*
climax 13
closed rehearsals 65; *see also* rehearsal schedule
color(s) coding 20, 28–30, 34
colored pencil 19, 29, 77
communicating plot 42; *see also* plot
communications 41–42
complication 13
contact list 70
Controls in Play Directing (Larry) 4

costume 18–19; elements 29; and make-up designers 80
Covey, S. 37
crisis 13
cues 11–12, 78; to cue 78; direct 73; importance of 53; indirect 73; light 44, 50, 52; master sheet 73; sound and music 19, 25, 29, 51; technical 20, 35, 36, 52
curtain calls 82

Dean, A. 4
Death of a Salesman (Miller) 6
designer presentations 42
dialogue/language/diction 11
direct cues 73; *see also* cues
director: first tasks 22; goals for 51; order of appearance 6–15; stage 16; stage manager and 66–84; technical 51–52, 77; units of 20; vision of 30
director's units 20, 25–27
distillation 22–24
Downstage Right 44
dress rehearsals 49, 50–54, 80; *see also* rehearsal schedule
duties of stage manager 67–68; *see also* stage manager

early rehearsal period 73–76; *see also* rehearsals
entrance-exit chart 71–72
Every Picture Tells a Story 11
exposition 10

fever chart 88, *89*
foreshadowing 10–11
Four One-Hundredths (Hellesen) 42, 85–125
Fundamentals of Play Direction (Carra) 3–4

The Glass Menagerie (Williams) 2, 5
Gogh, V. van 16
Gretzky, W. 37

ground plan 18
Guirgis, S. A. 7, 60

Harvard Drama Club 4
Hellesen, R. 85, 90–91
Hemingway, E. 22
house manager 80–82

Ibsen, H. 32
Ikkyu 6
inciting incident(s) 8, 90
indirect cues 73; *see also* cues

journal 19; notes 55; *see also* notes

Katselas, M. 127

later rehearsal period 76–78; *see also* rehearsal schedule
left column 19–20
left-hand pages 17, *18*, 30
lighting 19; cues and effects 29, 44, 50; designer 51
lines 22–23; *see also* redlining script
Loman, W. 6

The Man with the Flower in His Mouth (Pirandello) 3
meditation 6
Miller, A. 6
The Miser (Molière) 26–27
Molière 26–27
mood 14, 20
music/sounds of play 11, 28
music/spectacle 17–18

New York Times 31–32
notation symbols *57–60*
notes 55–57, *57–60*; *see also* journal notes; production

obstacle 13
order of appearance 6–15; antagonist 12; cast of characters 7; character five 8; climax 13; complication 13;

crisis 13; cues 11–12; dialogue/language/diction 11; exposition 10; foreshadowing 10–11; given circumstances 8–10; inciting incident(s) 8; mood 14; music/sounds of play 11; play's main dramatic question 13; play's main statement 14; playwright 7; plot 8; point of attack 12–13; production history 7; protagonist 12; resolution 13; the setting 8; spectacle/sights of play 11; style 14–15; subject/theme/thought 10; title 7; tone 14
Our Lady of 121st Street (Guirgis) 7, 60–64
over-rehearsed production 39

paper blocking 34, 46; *see also* blocking
Parks, Suzan-Lori 35
patience 50
performance: after 82; before 80–81; curtain calls 82; during acts 81; intermission 82; stage manager 80–83
photographs 82–83
physical movement 29
pick up rehearsals 54–55; *see also* rehearsal schedule
Pirandello, L. 3
play: main dramatic question 13, 91; main statement 14
playwright, 1, 7; elements of, 91; right-hand page, 36; scenes, 25; text of, 31, 32, 44; title of play, 7; words of, 1, 2, 30, 48
plot 8, 17; outline 17, 86–87; preliminary costume 72; preliminary lighting 72–73; preliminary property 72; preliminary sound 72
point of attack 12–13
poststrike responsibilities 83–84
preliminary blocking 20
preliminary costume plot 72
preliminary lighting plot 72–73
preliminary master cue sheet 73
preliminary property plot 72
preliminary sound plot 72
pretechnical rehearsal 76–78; *see also* rehearsal schedule
production: history 7; meetings 19; notes 56; photographs 82–83; schedules 37

program copy 76
prompt book: for artistic success 37–65; construction of 16–21; director of 2; electronic formats 16–17; overview 1–2; physical 16–17; research 17; template for director 2; well-conceived/constructed 2, 15
prompt script 71
properties 19, 29
property list 72
protagonist 12
protagonist's goal 12, 91

read through 73–74
redlining script 22–24
rehearsal schedule 19, 37–40, 69–70; blocking 74–76; closed 65; designer presentations 42; development and execution of 38; dress 80; pick up 54–55; pretechnical 76–78; quality of 37–38; reports 19; review 46–47; run 48; sample 60–64; staging 43–47; table 73–74; table work 41–43; technical 78–79; technical and dress 49, 50–54; in theatre 37; well-planned 38; work 47–50
research 17
resolution 12–13, 88, 91
reversal 13
review rehearsal 46–47; *see also* rehearsal schedule
right-hand pages 17, 35–36
Rohe, Mies Van der 16
Roth, J. 126
run rehearsals 48; *see also* rehearsal schedule

sample rehearsal guidelines 64–65; *see also* rehearsal schedule
sample rehearsal schedule 60–64; *see also* rehearsal schedule
scene designer 77
scene purpose 20
scenery 18
scenic elements 29
schedules: as blueprint 39; effective and dynamic 40; production 37; rehearsal 19, 37–40; rigidity of 39; well-planned 38
scripts 11–12, 15, 68–69; color coding 28; copies of 17; original 17; prompt 71; redlining 22–24
the setting 8
Shakespeare, W. 32, 35, 39

short-hand system 36
sights/spectacle of play 29
sound and music cues 19, 25, 29
sounds/music of play 28; *see also* music/sounds of play
spectacle/sights of play 11, 29
stage director 16
stage manager 52; auditions 69; contact list 70; director and 66–84; dress rehearsals 80; duties of 67–68; early rehearsal period 73–76; first technical rehearsal 78; later rehearsal period 76–78; performance 80–83; poststrike responsibilities 83–84; prerehearsal period 68; prompt script 71; rehearsal schedule 69–70; scripts 68–69; second technical rehearsal 79; strike 83; technical plots 71–73; *see also* assistant stage manager
staging rehearsals 43–47; blocking phase 46; review rehearsals 46–47; run rehearsals 48; *see also* rehearsal schedule
Stewart, R. 11
strike 83
style of play 14–15
Suzuki, T. 15

table rehearsals 73–74; *see also* rehearsal schedule
table work 41–43
technical cues 20, 35–36, 52
technical director 51–52, 77–79, 82; *see also* director
technical plots 71–73; *see also* plot
technical rehearsals 49, 50–54, 78–79; *see also* rehearsal schedule
three column left-hand page *18*, **21**, 31–34; adjectives and adverbs 33; column one 31–32; column three 32; column two 32; first steps 33–34; mood 33; objectives 33; purpose 33; title 33
three column work 19–21, *92–125*
title 7, 20, 33
tone 7, 11, 14

Williams, T. 2, 32
Wilson, R. 14–15
work rehearsals 47–50; *see also* rehearsal schedule

Yale School of Drama 4

For Product Safety Concerns and Information please contact our EU
representative GPSR@taylorandfrancis.com
Taylor & Francis Verlag GmbH, Kaufingerstraße 24, 80331 München, Germany

www.ingramcontent.com/pod-product-compliance
Lightning Source LLC
Chambersburg PA
CBHW080412300426
44113CB00015B/2495